DEAD ENDS OR DESTINY

*Seven Paths through the
Wilderness Experiences of Life*

W. Scott Moore

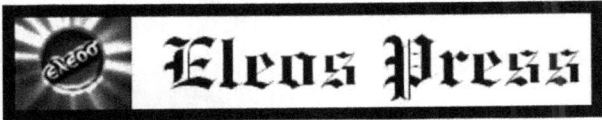

Eleos Press

Rogersville, Alabama

First Edition

Dead Ends or Destiny?

Author: W. Scott Moore, B.B.A, M.Div., D.Min.
© 2012 by Eleos Press www.eleospress.com

Cover Art: W. Scott Moore
Cover Design: **create**space™ and W. Scott Moore
Interior Formatting: Eleos Press www.eleospress.com
Also available in eBook form

Unless otherwise noted, all "Scripture quotations taken from the New American Standard Bible®, Copyright © 1960, 1962, 1963, 1968, 1971, 1972, 1973, 1975, 1977, 1995 by The Lockman Foundation. Used by permission." (www.Lockman.org)

ISBN-13: 978-0615587479

PRINTED IN THE UNITED STATES OF AMERICA

What Others Have Said

Denise George (cdwg@aol.com), author of 26 books, co-teacher of Boot Camps for Christian Writers:

In his new book, <u>Dead Ends or Destiny? Seven Paths Through the Wilderness Experiences of Life</u>, author Scott Moore teaches valuable lessons about "the wilderness" in a unique and highly-creative way! I found the book a delight to read, marveled at its creativity in teaching, and I learned much about spending time "in the wilderness." I highly recommend it.

Ellen C. Maze, author of <u>Rabbit: Chasing Beth</u> (Cullman, AL, United States) :

Author Scott Moore takes a little bit of the "devil's advocate" to parlay some very important biblical truths. A new way to find understanding in some of the most basic tenets in our Christian walk. I enjoy Moore's work, and I will definitely keep seeking him out. 5-stars for a very talented writer with a rare perspective.

Louise E. Wheeler (Atlanta, GA):

I wasn't sure what to expect when I purchased this book. I was pleasantly surprised that the story and format held my attention. This book explains parts of the bible in a story format that not only explained the bible but brought the relevance of the bible to today's time.... Highly recommend.

This book is dedicated to our three wonderful children: Mike, Kelly, and Susanna. And to our three precious grandchildren: Ashleigh, Abigail, and Kathryn.

FOREWORD

W. Scott Moore, in his book <u>Dead Ends or Destiny: Seven Paths through the Wilderness Experience of Life</u>, offers an interesting look into the life of the church as compared to the people of Israel as they wandered in the wilderness. He writes about familiar individuals in their desert journey toward the Promised Land and he gives the reader a unique look into the hearts and possible motives of each one. The story of God's people as they wandered in the wilderness has always given a vivid picture of life lived outside of the promises of God and life lived in disobedience to His word. It is a story of God's great love for His people as demonstrated through His mighty acts to bring them out of slavery into the land of Promise. The land of Promise is a picture of the place where they could truly live as God's children in victory over their enemies; a place where blessings would characterize their lives as they lived out obedience to the statutes of their God. Tested in the wilderness, the people failed to follow God's commands and thus remained in the wilderness, some never to experience the promises and inheritance given to them. We, too, can fail to experience the promises and blessings of God in our own wilderness experience. The Biblical story of the wilderness wanderings of Israel was written for our instruction so we would not follow the path of those who went before us in disobedience, but instead to follow the path of those who followed the Lord fully.

Scott has given us an intimate look into the lives of some who walked in obedience and others who did not. He has connected the lives of God's people, from the wilderness to the church, as they have followed similar paths through the centuries. It is a clarion call to the church today to heed the story of God's people as they wandered in the desert and as they walked according to their own ways suffering the consequences of an unclaimed inheritance. It is a cry for the church to take a look at the true condition of her heart and to respond to her God in complete obedience so that she can be all that God has called for her to be, and all that He has died for her to become.

Kathi Holcomb, Director
The Bethany Retreat Lodge
P.O. Box 513
Russellville, AL 35653
holcombbk@charter.net

The Bethany Retreat Lodge is a ministry of the Bethany Hope Center, "a refuge and a lighthouse for people who are hurting, and for people who want to grow in Christ through Biblical studies, support groups, retreats, conferences, and camps." For more information, visit: www.thebethanyhopecenter.com.

CONTENTS

INTRODUCTION

What is the Wilderness? Merriam-Webster[1] defined it as:

a: (1): a tract or region uncultivated and uninhabited by human beings (2): an area essentially undisturbed by human activity together with its naturally developed life community, b: an empty or pathless area or region, c: a part of a garden devoted to wild growth.

The primary antonym for "Wilderness" is "civilization." Synonyms for the word

---

[1] MERRIAM-WEBSTER'S COLLEGIATE DICTIONARY AND THESAURUS, DELUXE AUDIO EDITION®, Version 2.5, Copyright © Merriam-Webster, Incorporated, 47 Federal Street, P.O. Box 28l, Springfield, MA 01102.

"Wilderness" include:

- Badlands
- Barrenness
- Barrens
- Bleakness
- Bush
- Desert
- Dunes
- Emptiness
- Forest
- Outdoors
- Sand
- Timberland
- Tundra
- Wasteland
- Wild
- Woods

According to the Theological Wordbook of the Old Testament (TWOT), the word most frequently translated as "Wilderness" in the Old Testament is: מדבר (midbar). The authors of TWOT translated the word to mean "pasture, uninhabited land, or large tracts of Wilderness."[2]

It doesn't sound like a very pleasant place, does it? And yet, God wants you to go there. And, as you begin your Christian life, He will *send* you there. How do I know? Listen to the words of Jesus in Matthew 10:24: "A disciple is not above his teacher, nor a slave above his master." Christ Himself spent 40 days and nights in the Wilderness. If it was good enough for Him, it will be good enough for you and good enough for me.

The good news is that the Wilderness is the place of God's *provision* for your life. He sent manna from Heaven for the Israelites; He provided them with water. Their clothes and sandals lasted for forty years; the garments grew as the children grew. God sent the angels to minister to Jesus at the end of His forty-day wilderness experience. He sent ravens daily to the brook Cherith to feed Elijah.

What does it all mean? While you are in the Wilderness, God will supply all of your daily needs. He will hold your hand. And then He will

---

[2] R. Laird Harris, Gleason L. Archer, Jr., and Bruce K. Waltke, eds., Theological Wordbook of the Old Testament, (Chicago: Moody Press, 1980).

send you into the Promised Land—the place of *partnership* with Him. Provision before partnership—that sounds like a wonderful plan!

Stories in the Pentateuch, or first five books of the Bible, most clearly define God's concept of the Wilderness. For the purpose of this book *Egypt* will represent the world, the *Red Sea* will represent salvation, the *Wilderness* will represent spiritual immaturity, the *Jordan River* will represent the decision to live the Spirit-filled life, and the *Promised Land* will represent the Christian life as led by the Holy Spirit.

The World

"The world" is not so much a place as it is a concept; it is an order of things—a system, if you will, in opposition to God and His kingdom. The place we will leave on our journey into the Wilderness, Egypt, is a picture of "the world." Pharaoh fancied himself to be a god. He believed his will could, and would, overrule the will of Jehovah God. He and his vast army found out differently at the Red Sea!

The world is ever-present in this life. Many Christians believe that, by leaving Egypt, we will be leaving the world behind. They are definitely wrong!

Your first battle as a new believer in Jesus Christ will be with "the world." You will regularly fight the urge, that so many of your contemporaries will embrace, to return to Egypt.

Salvation

The Red Sea represents salvation, or deliverance. God delivers us out of the kingdom of the world—Egypt—and into the kingdom of God. God has sent His Deliverer, namely, Jesus Christ. Those of us that follow Him by faith out of *the world* receive His salvation; His deliverance. We are transferred from the kingdom of darkness into His wonderful kingdom of light!

Spiritual Immaturity

The Wilderness is the place of spiritual immaturity—the land of spiritual infants. It has been designed by God to be a stop along the way for those Christians that will desire to walk daily with Jesus Christ. For many it has become the home, the spiritual nursery, in which believers, refusing to grow up, play church together.

You may ask, "Why would anyone want to *stay* in the Wilderness?" The answer is simple: it is the place where God *visibly* takes care of us in the same way as parents care for their infant children. He leads you and He feeds you. He performs miracles. His actions in your life are primarily *external*.

Sadly, the *majority* of God's people don't want to grow up; they want to remain in God's nursery. They are described in Hebrews 5:12:

> *For though by this time you ought to be teachers, you have need again for someone to teach you the elementary principles of the oracles of God, and you have come to need milk and not solid food.*

These people have been Christians long enough to have matured spiritually; instead, they have signed up to receive their spiritual "welfare benefits"; they have grown to expect that God, and their pastor, will do everything *for* them.

At some point, however, God wants you to grow up and to mature. He wants to form a *partnership* with you. He wants to work *inside* of your life to transform you; His actions, at that point in time, will become primarily *invisible*.

Seven People You Will Meet in the Wilderness

This book consists of seven vignettes, describing the lives of seven characters from the Bible. Each character will teach you lessons that you will need in order to survive the Wilderness experiences of your life. They are the evil talebearer, the radical nonconformist, the juvenile delinquent, the overwhelmed pastor, the unwilling immigrant, the lone ranger, and the silent partner.

Why will you meet them in that order? They are ranked from the least helpful to the most helpful to you in handling your Wilderness experience. Each one will post his résumé, describe his life, and share his epitaph. They will each issue the same invitation: "follow *me*."

Is There a Shortcut — an Alternate Path?

You may never have imagined that the dismal place you are now entering could become your pathway to paradise. I have concluded that God's plan for every believer is to take them through the Wilderness on their journey to a much better place. You ask, "*Every* believer?" Yes. God's plan for *every* believer includes a trip through the Wilderness.

Here is why I make that assertion. Millions of men and women, boys and girls came out of Egypt in what is now called, "The Exodus." I will ask you two questions: 1) "How many of them were 'given a pass?'" and 2) "How many of them were allowed to go directly into the Promised Land without first passing through the Wilderness?" The answer to both questions is, as I am sure you know, *none* of them. They *all* traveled through it — even the two "innocent parties" — Joshua and Caleb.

The question you may be asking (I know I

have certainly asked it on several occasions) is, "Why? Why do we have to go through a place of pain and suffering, of misery and sadness, before we reach the Promised Land?" You won't like my answer any more than I want to give it: because it is God's plan, His will.

But here's the good news. Your choices and your actions will determine the length of time that you will stay there. Every one of your contemporaries, except a handful, will live out the remainder of their lives in the Wilderness. But, my dear friend, God is offering you a marvelous alternative!

Here is the all-important question. Will you join with Jesus and the *next generation* — those under the control of His Holy Spirit — as He leads us across "the River," and as we claim this world for Him?

THE EVIL TALEBEARER

I assume you have read through your Bible. Let me introduce myself. My name is Gaddi, meaning "my fortune." Why should you follow me? Because leadership is influence. And I have an *enormous* amount of influence. In fact, my influence will go beyond the grave and continue to be evident in the lives of my people for four decades!

Additionally, you will likely discover that my counterparts continue to be alive and well in *your* church today, as well.

My Résumé

My personal résumé, for your consideration, is as follows:

- I am the son of Susi of the tribe of

Manasseh.

- I am a member of an elite group that includes the likes of Shammua the son of Zaccur of the Israelite tribe of Reuben. You haven't heard of him? Have you heard about Shaphat, the son of Hori, of the tribe of Simeon? Igal, the son of Joseph, of the tribe of Issachar? Then surely you must have heard of Palti, the son of Raphu, of the tribe of Benjamin? Gaddiel, the son of Sodi, of the tribe of Zebulun? Ammiel, the son of Gemalli, of the tribe of Dan? Sethur, the son of Michael, of the tribe of Asher? Nahbi, the son of Vophsi, of the tribe of Naphtali? And last but not least, Geuel, the son of Machi, of the tribe of Gad? Okay, what about Oshea, also known as Joshua, and Caleb the son of Jephunneh of the tribe of Judah?

- Oh, you have heard of *them*, but you still don't know who *I* am? I am the spokesman for the majority of the twelve spies that crossed "the River" — our name for the *Jordan* River — and then returned to the encampment with our report.

The Majority Report

As I have said, my name is Gaddi. My name, as you will soon discover, *should* have been מַעַל — ma'al: "the *un*faithful one." No matter how many miracles that God will perform, I simply will not believe.

I may be the representative from the *smallest* tribe in Israel, Manasseh, but I can proudly say that I am in the majority. You ask, "The majority? Aren't you Israelites supposed to be living in a *theo*cracy?"[3]

I reply, "Are you kidding? We all know that God isn't *really* supposed to rule in the lives of His people. The world has invented something better that we call a '*dem*ocracy' — a place where the majority rules. And, since I can easily mislead most of the people, I enjoy living in a democracy."

Anachronistically, Abraham Lincoln put it well: "You can fool all of the people some of the time and some of the people all of the time." I don't like the rest of his quotation: "But you can't

---

[3] A country ruled by God.

fool all of the people all of the time." But no matter; I will get *my* way *most* of the time!

I will let you in on a little secret: there are no such things as either true democracies or genuine congregational governments. Someone good or evil (usually evil), will *always* rise to the top and place himself or herself in charge of the rest of the group. But, since Israel has chosen to become "democratic," I can displace God's leader — Moses — and lead the people where *I* want them to go. Isn't this great?

So I "worked the crowds." You may be familiar with this practice in the New Testament. One day the people were crying, "Hosanna"; the next day my spiritual descendants, the Pharisees, inspired them to chant, "Crucify Him!" I love it!

Another secret: I don't like Moses. He is *God's* choice. I will make it my mission in life to thwart his control. I will rule this nation. I will be in charge.

We returned from our excursion into the Promised Land. Moses ran to greet us. He looked at Joshua as he asked, "How was it?" Joshua replied, "Even more beautiful than you could imagine!"

"That's great," Moses said, as he proceeded to make a serious mistake. He called the entire assembly together to hear the "majority report." Only two spies disagreed with *me* — or should I say, with *us*. Since there were five times as many of us as there are of them, *our* report carried more weight than *their* report.

I began, "Everything God told us about Canaan was true. It is beautiful, and the resources are plentiful. We would have all that we need to take care of our families — and more!" Moses and all the people smiled. I continued, "But." And then Moses' countenance began to fade. He thought to himself, "Here it comes. I hate that word, 'but!' 'But,' 'however,' and 'nevertheless' are three dishonest words."

No matter what I have said prior to "but" will be nullified by that little word. Moses mused, "Gaddi might as well have moved right to his next point without the lead-in. He doesn't really believe that God has told us the truth."

"But," I continued, "we can't go into that land. The land of Canaan is inhabited by monsters! Even the cities themselves are huge!"

I had conspired with Geuel from the tribe of Gad to be the next person to speak. He picked up my lament as he said to Moses, "You can listen to the reports from Caleb and Joshua if you like. But (he said slowly for effect) i f   y o u   d o ,   w e   w i l l   *a l l*   b e   k i l l e d." He turned to look at the people. He stretched out his hands as he declared, "I don't know about the rest of you, but as for me and my house—*we're* not going back over there."

I couldn't have said it better myself. His comment was so powerfully worded that it would inspire Joshua to make a similar, though very distinct, remark in the distant future.[4]

Moses looked on with horror as the color literally began to drain from the faces of every person in the crowd. He would see that ghastly look again on the face of his sister: leprosy! This leprosy, however, was of a spiritual nature. An entire nation was being defeated before his eyes,

---

[4] Joshua 24:15.

even before the first battle would begin.

I *Almost* Became the Leader

All night long the people wept. "Why did God do this to us? Why did He bring us out here to die?"

The next morning, I assembled the other nine members of "the ten." I said, "We have to do something. We can't allow Moses to lead us across 'the River.' We will all die."

Zaccur, from the tribe of Reuben, asked, "Then what should we do?" I rolled my eyes as I responded, "We have to turn back."

Hori from the tribe of Simeon raised his hand. I nodded at him. He asked, "Who will lead us? I doubt Moses will agree to take us back to Egypt."

I am experienced in the "humble look." I answered Hori by saying, "I am probably the *least* qualified, since I am from the smallest tribe in Israel. But I am willing to risk my life by moving to the front of the procession. I am willing to lead us as we face whatever obstacles or dangers we may encounter."

"The nine" all nodded in agreement. We would return to Egypt, and I would be the leader.

Ammiel from the tribe of Dan asked, "What should we do with Moses and Aaron?" I said, "We will have to kill them. Look around you at all the rocks. What comes to mind?"

Ammiel's eyes begin to narrow. I could see that he and I were "on the same page." He asked, "You think we should *stone* them?" I replied, allowing him to take the credit for the proposal, "That is a great idea!"

We carefully maneuvered ourselves into the various parts of the crowd, like a serpent silently wriggling towards its prey. Everyone agreed with us—we would stone Aaron and Moses and then the others would all follow *me* back to Egypt. Remember: we are a *dem*ocracy rather than a *theo*cracy; the majority rules.[5]

My, I mean, Ammiel's, perfect plan was coming together—perfectly. Nothing, or so I thought, could stop us now. Suddenly, God's glory appeared in the tent of meeting. We all saw it; we were all terrified! The Lord told Moses, "I

---

[5] Numbers 14.

have the solution. I will kill all of *them* and make a great nation from your family."

Moses, as usual, interceded on our behalf. God, as a result, spared us. Moses is a better man than I. I would have told Him to "go for it"; Moses didn't. Mysteriously, in spite of all that we have done, or will do, to him —he will still manage to love and to serve us.

I "Repent"

Have you ever read Hebrews 6:1-8? Scholars in your day will be puzzled as to the meaning of the passage. I can help them. I believe the writer is referring to me:

> *Therefore leaving the elementary teaching about the Christ, let us press on to maturity, not laying again a foundation of repentance from dead works and of faith toward God, of instruction about washings and laying on of hands, and the resurrection of the dead and eternal judgment. And this we will do, if God permits. For in the case of those who have once been enlightened and have tasted of the*

heavenly gift and have been made partakers of the Holy Spirit, and have tasted the good word of God and the powers of the age to come, and then have fallen away, it is impossible to renew them again to repentance, since they again crucify to themselves the Son of God and put Him to open shame. For ground that drinks the rain which often falls on it and brings forth vegetation useful to those for whose sake it is also tilled, receives a blessing from God; but if it yields thorns and thistles, it is worthless and close to being cursed, and it ends up being burned.

I have walked across with the other spies into the Promised Land. I have seen the wonderful blessings that God intended for us to enjoy. I have "tasted of the heavenly gift." But I have turned back in my heart toward the Wilderness and, ultimately, Egypt. I refuse to go in. And, as you and I will soon see, I no longer can.

Moses told us the bad news. As a result of our disobedience, all of the people twenty years old and above were doomed to die in the wilderness. Hey, wait a minute; that includes *me*!

And our children will have to spend forty years in the Wilderness before *they* will be allowed to enter into Canaan.[6]

I waved my hands excitedly, Moses finally noticed me. "Yes, Gaddi," he said. I ran up to him and bowed at his feet. In an act of feigned repentance I said, "Moses, I am so sorry. I never should have prevented the people from going in. It is my fault. Let's go!"

Moses asked, "Go where?" I replied, "Into the Promised Land."

Moses looked sadly at me. "I'm sorry, Gaddi. God has closed and sealed that door of opportunity — at least for now."

I dismissed Moses' statement. "Come on everyone," I shouted. I watched as Moses and his allies — Aaron, Caleb, and Joshua — turned their backs and walked away.

The "real" men and I laughed at Moses and his company as we marched across "the River" into Canaan. I thought, "This will be a breeze. We don't need Moses' help; in fact, we

---

[6] Numbers 14:26-35.

don't even need *God*. We can do this!"[7]

We began running toward the Promised Land with our swords in our hands. I can't really say, "We." Brave leader that I have always been, I placed myself squarely at the back lines and sent the others ahead. I shouted for the rest of the group to follow. We had no sooner reached the base of the hill when the Amalekites and Canaanites descended upon us, as Moses' would later recount, "like a swarm of bees."

I shouted, "Retreat!" We survivors ran all the way to Hormah; we wept again over another defeat. The thought we all shared was, "How could God do this to us?" Looking back, I guess we really did it to ourselves. Like Esau in Hebrews 12:17b, "[We were] rejected, for [we] found no place for repentance, though [we] sought for it with tears." My entire generation discovered a principle the hard way: you can never return to the Promised Land, the Holy Spirit controlled life, once you have experienced it and have *willingly* returned to the Wilderness!

No wonder so many of the church members of your day will be so complacent—so

---

[7] Deuteronomy 1:41-46.

indifferent—when they hear about the "abundant life" Jesus has prepared for them.[8] He will accurately describe the people of your day in Luke 9:62, "No one, after putting his hand to the plow and looking back, is fit for the kingdom of God."

My Epitaph

The description of my death and the deaths of the other members of "the ten" are found in Numbers 14:36-37:

> As for the men whom Moses sent to spy out the land and who returned and made all the congregation grumble against him by bringing out a bad report concerning the land, even those men who brought out the very bad report of the land died by a plague before the Lord.

How shall I describe the plague? As background, perhaps you have read of the death of the wicked queen, Jezebel. 2 Kings 9:35 states: "They went to bury her, but they found nothing

---

[8] John 10:10.

more of her than the skull and the feet and the palms of her hands." A famous preacher will one day proclaim a sermon entitled, "Payday Someday."[9] He will describe the death of Jezebel in the following terms:

> *God Almighty saw to it that the hungry dogs despised the brains that conceived the plot that took Naboth's life. God Almighty saw to it that the mangy lean dogs of the back alleys despised the hands that wrote the plot that took Naboth's life. God Almighty saw to it that the lousy dogs which ate carrion despised the feet that walked in Baal's courts and then in Naboth's vineyard.*

In the same way, this plague *slowly* targeted the parts of our bodies that were primarily involved in our bad report and subsequent rebellion. Because we refused to see the land through the eyes of faith, we all went blind. Because we gave a bad report and later spoke against Moses, our tongues began to swell

[9] Timothy George and Denise George, gen. eds., <u>Payday Someday and Other Sermons by Robert Greene Lee</u>, (Nashville: Broadman and Holman Publishers, 1995), pg. 48.

and to then to shrivel. Because we took up stones on one occasion to kill God's servants, our hands became blistered and sore. And since we had marched into Canaan against God's clear command, our feet and legs became infected; they eventually had to be amputated.

You may have heard someone make this statement regarding a suffering saint: "I am praying that the Lord will call her home." In other words, they are asking God to end her pain and take her home to be with Him in Heaven.

Caleb ("the Dog") once laughingly said, as he pointed at me and at the other members of "the ten" — "I wish the *devil* would call them home." I don't know about Moses' prayers, but I am fairly confident that *Caleb's* prayers were answered on the day of our passing. Unfortunately for us, the *real* suffering, eternal agony, was just beginning!

My *least* favorite name for God has been Jehovah-shammah, meaning "God is there." I had the opportunity to meet with Him in the Promised Land, but I refused to go.

As you march around the wilderness, you will have the opportunity to read my tombstone on several occasions. It aptly reads "Gaddi — Evil

Talebearer—He Never Made It and He Kept the Rest of Us from Going In."

Even though I am gone, I still have many followers to this day. In fact, I may have inspired one of your modern day recreational sports. You tell me. When the other members of "the ten" and I died of the plague, they buried us and placed our tombstones in the following configuration:

Gaddi

Somebody, possibly Caleb, took a mental picture of the configuration and formulated an idea. He arranged some tall, thin stones and narrowed the pattern somewhat. And then he took one of the round stones that are so plentiful in Palestine and *threw* it at the other rocks.

Several fell down.

This man, possibly Caleb, had a better idea. He began to *roll* the round stone; a larger number of the tall, thin stones fell. He found that if he put a little reverse spin on the round stone and struck the first upright stone in just the right place — representing my tombstone in the original configuration — he could actually knock them all down at one time.

What is the name of the sport? I think it may now be known as "tenpins" or, rather, "bowling."

Nevertheless, I invite you to "FOLLOW ME!"

THE RADICAL

NONCONFORMIST

My name is Dathan. I want you to follow me. I have been with Moses for forty years. And, after four decades together, I am still not convinced. He is still "on trial" with me. He has fooled many of the others, but he hasn't fooled me—I can see right through him. He doesn't have any idea where he's going.

What a joke! We follow some puff of smoke around all day long and a giant torch at night. Are you kidding me? Moses is lost and he's taking us with him. Not if *I* can help it.

My Résumé

My personal résumé, for your consideration, is as follows:

My Accomplishments:

- I am a member of the tribe of Reuben.
- I am the chief lobbyist for the opposition party.
- I have, over time, (forty years) developed a large retinue.
- I enjoy working in the background—I am most effective wh-en people are unaware that I am personally involved.
- I am patient. Unlike Gaddi, the "Evil Talebearer," I have waited patiently for the

right time to assume control.

My Objective:

- My name means "belonging to a fountain." My goal is to live up to my name — to be a refreshing fountain of water in a dry and thirsty land. I think back upon Elim. You remember: that wonderful place with the twelve springs of water. I despised Moses for leading us away from there and into this horrific desert. But, one day, I will have my opportunity to lead a rebellion. Although it will be a difficult task, I will systematically turn the hearts of millions of people against their leader!

My Method

As a lobbyist, my first convert has been my brother, Abiram. He was easy to convince — we have both felt, for years, that Moses has failed all of us as a leader.

I then persuaded my kids to help rally

their contemporaries, the second generation Wilderness wanderers, to our cause. You know — those people that Moses said would be allowed to enter into the Promised Land after my generation dies off. But I have other plans for them — both generations will inhabit the land together on *this* side of "the River."

These youngsters agree with me — we are *not* going to cross over into a place inhabited by giants. What in the world was this man, this *Moses*, thinking?

I then incited the Korahites to challenge Moses' and Aaron's credentials to lead the people. What a thing of beauty — I made everything appear to be a family matter (Moses and Korah are both from the tribe of Levi)! The Korahites, under my tutelage, approached Moses and basically said, "Just who do you think you are? We are all equal here. You are no better than any one of the rest of us."

You may ask, "So — what was your modus operandi?" "How did you accomplish your goals?"

- I reveled in the praises of others.
- I fancied myself as being better qualified to lead the assembly than the pastor.
- I was a constant wedge between the pastor and the other leaders; I accomplished my objectives by talking negatively about the pastor to the leaders, and vice-verse.
- I both listened to, and encouraged, all malicious gossip that others spread about our pastor.
- I meticulously "tested the waters" by taking others aside to ask their opinions regarding our pastor's suitability to lead — or lack thereof.
- I wisely dropped the conversation when confronted. However, I added the names of those who disagreed with me to my list of *future* targets.
- There are two types of people — talkers and doers. I have always been a talker. I really have never worked at all; I have been one of the laziest people you would have ever met. I have survived by taking the credit

for the work that others were doing.

- People have mistakenly thought that I could be trusted. They placed their confidence in me and listened to my recommendations; I was so convincing that they even rejected godly counsel in favor of my false counsel.

My motto: never do anything yourself that you can incite someone else into doing. That way, if there is a backlash, you walk away scot-freely. Or so I thought.[10]

My Biblical Counterparts

I will tell you my personal story a little later in this chapter. But, first, let me introduce you to my Biblical counterparts. The Bible accounts, as I am sure you realize, are filled with people who will be just like me. Two in particular will go down in my personal Noncomformist Hall of Fame: Doeg the Edomite and Absalom,

---

[10] Numbers 16:1-3.

the son of David.

Doeg the Edomite

I am sure you have heard of Doeg the Edomite. Doeg was the chief of King Saul's shepherds.

Shepherding is supposed to be a 24 hours a day, seven days a week job. Not for Doeg. The other shepherds did all of his work for him while he sat around in the coffee shop all day until "quitting time."

One day David and some men walked into the Espresso Palace. They wanted to speak confidentially with Amilech the priest. Doeg was bored, so he eavesdropped on their conversation. And then he reported everything back to Saul.

Saul was distraught after hearing Doeg's story. He fumbled with his spear as he reflected upon the times when he had attempted to kill David in the palace. He mentally placed a bull's eye over David's heart. He could almost see the spear leaving his own hand and entering into the center of his target.

He looked around the room, pathetically.

He thought, "No one cares about me." He said, "I know you like David more than you like me; my own son has turned against me. But don't forget: *I* am the one that has taken care of all of you; *I* have made you rich and have given you your cushy jobs. Please tell me. To whom did David speak in the coffee shop?"

There was silence in the room for several minutes. Finally, my friend Doeg answered his question. "Oh great king, David spoke with Ahimilech the priest. Ahimilech prayed with, and for, David; he gave him some loaves of the Bread of the Presence to eat, and Goliath's sword for protection."[11]

I see the light is beginning to come on for many of you — you now understand that Doeg is the man that informed Saul of David's whereabouts. But there's more.[12]

Saul led his entourage into the coffee shop; he confronted Ahimilech for helping David. Ahimilech didn't have a clue that he had done anyting wrong. He said, "David is a good man and a great warrior. Not only that — he's *your* son-

[11] 1 Samuel 22:6-10.
[12] 1 Samuel 22:14-19.

in-law. I don't know what you are so upset about."

Saul became even more enraged. He shouted, "Ahimilech, I am going to kill you and all the members of your family!" He commanded his guards to carry out the sentence of death; they refused. They guards trembled as they asked one another, "Is he telling us to kill God's priests? We can't do that!"

Saul looked on with pitiful eyes as he whined to Doeg, "Would you do it for me? Please?" Doeg smiled wryly as he rose from his chair. Before anyone had time to react, Doeg's hungry sword tasted the flesh of Ahimilech's abdomen. Not satisfied, he turned to another priest. And then another, until eighty-five men of God were lying in a virtual crimson river of their own blood. He didn't stop there — he went into the homes of the priests. He killed their wives, their children, even their livestock. His master was pleased. And so am I.

Now you're thinking, "This Doeg is a rough character." What an understatement — he was so evil that he rated an entire Psalm! Turn to Psalm 52, beginning with the introductory statement: "For the choir director. A Maskil of David, when Doeg the Edomite came and told Saul and said to him, 'David has come to the house of Ahimelech.'"

Now look at the rest of the Psalm:

Why do you boast in evil, O mighty man? The lovingkindness of God endures all day long. Your tongue devises destruction, like a sharp razor, O worker of deceit. You love evil more than good, falsehood more than speaking what is right. Selah. You love all words that devour, O deceitful tongue. But God will break you down forever; He will snatch you up and tear you away from your tent, and uproot you from the land of the living. Selah. The righteous will see and fear, and will laugh at him, saying, "Behold, the man who would not make God his refuge, but trusted in the abundance of his riches and was strong in his evil desire." But as for me, I am like a green olive tree in the house of God; I trust in the lovingkindness of God forever and ever. I will give You thanks forever, because You have done it, and I will wait on Your name, for it is good, in the presence of Your godly ones.

Here is Doeg's résumé:

- He listens to the private conversations of others.
- He is loyal to an ungodly constituency.
- He is boastful and proud.
- He is a tattletale.
- He has no fear of God.
- He is willing to destroy God's servants and their families.
- He is a liar.
- He is caustic and abrasive.

As I said, Doeg is my kind of guy!

Absalom

Absalom is the other member of my Nonconformist Hall of Fame. Saul had been defeated; David was now on the throne. David had grown accustomed to being king, and was now enjoying its "benefits." Consequently, he made a new "friend with benefits" as he committed adultery with Bathsheba. He then attempted to cover up his act by murdering her husband, Uriah the Hittite, one of his most loyal subjects.[13] Nathan, the prophet, confronted David; David repented. Nevertheless, David would ultimately suffer the *consequences* of his sins.[14]

One of David's sons, Amnon, fell in love, or rather lust, with his half-sister, Tamar. Upon the advice of Jonadab, Amnon pretended to be sick. He asked his father's permission for Tamar to come into his bedroom to feed him. When she arrived, he raped her. And then he sent her away in shame.

David did nothing in response. Tamar's brother, Absalom, took matters into his own hands. He killed Amnon, and fled to another country for three years.[15] After a series of events, Absalom returned to Jerusalem. David refused to meet with him for two years. Absalom utilized his time well by sitting in the gate; he intercepted people on their way to meet with David. He

---

[13] 2 Samuel 11.
[14] 2 Samuel 12:1-14.
[15] 2 Samuel 13.

would tell the people, "The king is extremely busy—he doesn't have time for you anymore. But *I* do."

And then he would listen. Genuinely listen. Listen reflectively. Listen intuitively. Listen craftily. He would conclude his meetings with this statement: "Life would be so much better for you if only *I* were your king."

He eventually won the hearts of the Israelites and turned them against his father. The popular term you will have for this phenomenon in your day will be that David had an "Absalom in the gate!"[16]

See what I mean? Absalom was a lobbyist par excellence—just like *me*. Here is Absalom's résumé:

- Deceptive—spends time with the masses pretending to be interested in meeting their needs.
- Good looking (like *me*).
- Eloquent—knows what to say and how to say it.
- Patient—waits for the right timing to

---

[16] 2 Samuel 15:1-6.

retaliate.

- Flamboyant—gives the appearance of being in control before he actually makes his overtures to assume the throne.

My Epitaph

The sons of Korah paid for their sin of presumptuousness with their own lives. God exposed our treachery toward Moses. My brother and I, therefore, would pay a much higher price than Korah—our family members would all die with us.

True to Moses' word, the ground opened up and fire came up from the earth; all of us, including our women and children, were consumed as we fell into the crevasse. The jaws of death consumed us. It was a horrible way to die!

My influence was so great that the people continued to rebel even after my death. They blamed Moses for the actions God had taken. God, in response to their criticism, sent a plague that killed almost 15,000 people, including the remainder of those that He had said must die before Israel could enter the Promised Land.

A common sin practiced by all generations will become known as *eisegesis*: "the interpretation of a text (as of the Bible) by reading into it one's own ideas."[17] Many of you, my dear readers, have adopted a common misinterpretation of the first part of Hebrews 9:27: "and inasmuch as it is appointed for men to die once." The word translated "appointment" simply means "awaiting." Death, for the living, is obviously something that is "awaiting" them in the future.

Many of your contemporaries ("armchair theologians," I like to call them) will tell you that the verse means that the time of your death has been previously set in Heaven by God Himself — we all have, as they will tell you, an "appointment with death." Nothing could be further from the truth. Have you forgotten the fifteen years God added to Hezekiah's life in response to his

---

[17] MERRIAM-WEBSTER'S COLLEGIATE DICTIONARY AND THESAURUS, DELUXE AUDIO EDITION®, Version 2.5, Copyright © Merriam-Webster, Incorporated, 47 Federal Street, P.O. Box 28l, Springfield, MA 01102.

request?[18]

And, just as surely as God can add to your life, He can also shorten it just as dramatically. You may be thinking, "God knew in advance that you would lead the insurrection against Moses; He, therefore, had already determined the time and means of your death." That may possibly be so. But, I ask you, "Other than following my leadership, what did my wife and children do wrong?" And yet they perished with me. My choices shortened not only my life, but also theirs.

Have I convinced you? Don't tell me that, after you have heard my story, you still hold to the "appointment with death" concept. Have you heard of my friends, Ananias and Sapphira?[19] Here is the background.

People were converting to some heresy or spinoff from Judaism called "Christianity." As you might imagine, many of the new believers were carrying their new faith to the extreme; they were becoming fanatics. In fact, some of the newcomers in Jerusalem were selling all of their possessions and contributing the proceeds to one

---

[18] 2 Kings 20:1-6.
[19] Acts 5:1-11.

common treasury.

Ananias concocted a plan with his wife, Sapphira. "Honey," he said, "why don't we sell that piece of land your father left us? We're not using it anyway." Sapphira looked admiringly at him. She replied, "That's a good idea, sweetheart. What are we going to do with the money?"

"Well, Sapphira," Ananias continued, "I was thinking that we could buy that necklace that you have been staring at in the marketplace for weeks. We could give the rest of the money to the church. But there is only one problem."

She asked, "Problem? What is the problem?" He replied, "We won't fit in. Some of the folks are selling everything they have and giving huge amounts of money to the church."

"That *is* a problem," she replied. "What is your solution?" Ananias winked at her as he continued, "We could sell the land for one thousand denarii, buy your necklace for 200 denarii, and give the rest to the Lord. Eight hundred denarii is a good offering!"

"That's true, Ananias," Sapphira agreed. "And, since no one else would know, we could *tell* them that we sold the land for 800 denarii."

You know the rest of the story. Ananias walked up to Peter and handed him the money. He told Peter, "We sold a piece of land, and this is the full payment — 800 denarii."

Peter looked at him in anger. You know how preachers are: they always want your money! He said, "Are you *sure* this is this all of it?" Ananias grinned. "Yes Peter, this is all of it. Right down to the last denarius."

Peter shouted so that everyone in the room could hear. "You, Ananias, are a liar! And you haven't lied to *me*; you have lied to *God!*"

Ananias' life abruptly ended. His "appointment," like mine, came somewhat sooner than we had both expected. Some of the men picked up his already rigor mortised body, carried it outside to the adjoining church cemetery, and buried it.

Sapphira strutted in. She told the same lie. The Lord, once again, opened his appointment book. He saw that He had an immediate opening for *her*. And she died.

The choices you make, good or bad, will definitely have an effect upon your lifespan. But please don't listen to me. Please don't heed my warning. Just keep on disobeying God. Keep on openly rejecting His claims upon your life. It really won't make any difference whatsoever. And the good news is that you may have the opportunity to meet *me* much sooner than you had anticipated!

My *least* favorite name for God has been Jehovah-tsidkenu, "God our righteousness." Because He is holy and righteous, my family and I are forever separated from His presence.

My tombstone doesn't really exist. But the surviving Israelites have an engraved memorial they each carry in their mind that reads: "Dathan—Rebel Leader—Died Prematurely— Took His Entire Family with Him." My brother's tombstone and the tombstones of his wife and children are in the imaginary family plot—right next to mine.

Dathan

Nevertheless I, like Gaddi, also invite you to
"FOLLOW ME!"

THE JUVENILE

DELINQUENT

My name is Abidan. My name means, "My father is judge." My name *should* have been נער—nah' ar, which means "little boy." People like me just never seem to grow up.

Imagine a nursery run by the children—the babies are in charge! Now imagine you are the sole nursery worker. Do you find that concept a little far-fetched? I hardly think so. You see, our nursery worker's name is Moses. He is babysitting the twelve tribes of Israel—literally millions of people—as we travel through the Wilderness.

You probably have a similar nursery worker in your church that you disdainfully refer to as "Reverend." According to Adrian Rogers, there are many unusual babies in our local churches today. They don't eat anything all week long. The pastor force feeds them five gallons of milk every Sunday morning. He will pat them on their backs to burp them while he is shaking their hands on their way out of the church. Strange babies indeed!

My Résumé

My personal résumé, for your consideration, is as follows:

- I am the son of Gideoni.[20]
- I am referred to in Numbers 10:24 as "over the tribal army of the sons of Benjamin."
- I have become *the* leader for the majority of people you will meet in the Wilderness — the juvenile delinquents.
- My tribe is on the west side of the Israeli

---

[20] Numbers 1:11.

encampment.[21]

- I lead an army of 35,400 men.[22]
- I took my offering to the dedication of the altar on the ninth day.[23]
- I represent the largest constituency in the Wilderness. As I am sure that you know, bigger *always* means better. Millions of people believe just as I do. And that many people simply can't be wrong.

My Personal References:

- Elishama the son of Ammihud, leader of the tribe of Ephraim.
- Gamaliel the son of Pedahzur, leader of the sons of Manasseh.

My Mission: "I want my way!"

Have you ever noticed the way little children will act in order to gain their father's attention? Once you have understood that

---

[21] Numbers 2:18-22.
[22] Numbers 2:23.
[23] Numbers 7:60.

dynamic, you will have a fairly good handle on my actions toward my two primary leaders through the Wilderness: Moses *and* God.

I didn't really want to make Moses' life so miserable; as a child, I simply *loved* to complain. I was a "spin doctor" — I put a negative twist on whatever Moses said or did. He could not, under any circumstances, possibly win.

Moses led us out of Egypt to the Red Sea. We looked back and saw a cloud of dust coming our way: Pharaoh and the entire army of Egypt. I could almost see the headlines in the Cairo Gazette:

> **"Millions Die! No Israelites Escape Alive in Bloody Campaign! Entire Nation Obliterated by Our Beloved Pharaoh and his Vast Army."**

All night long we were writing our last wills and testaments — assigning our worldly possessions to the people we had all grown to love back in Egypt. One thing was for sure: we were going to die.

At the last minute Moses raised that rod of his—how I have grown to despise it. He raised his rod—now known as the "rod of God"—and the waters of the Red Sea parted in the middle. All night long a wind blew through the middle of the opening, drying the sea bed for us to cross in the morning.

God supernaturally delivered us from Pharaoh's army. We passed through the Red Sea on dry land, only to turn and watch the mighty waters as they returned in one great heap to engulf kings, soldiers, horses, and chariots.

I could immediately see that I was in trouble. The people would love Moses for this one. His miserable sister, Miriam, even wrote a ballad commemorating the event; the people excitedly sang the chorus.

I will bide my time. Moses will make a mistake, and I will make him pay.

No sooner had the people finished singing than they realized they needed water. Moses led us to a waterhole in the Wilderness of Shur. I tasted the water and spit it out on the ground. I waited until a crowd had gathered around.

"Taste it," I shouted. One by one, hundreds of people repeated my actions. They tried a mouthful and spit it out. I began to slowly chant, "B i t t e r ,   b i t t e r , this water tastes b i t t e r !" The others picked up the refrain; they soon liked my ditty even better than Miriam's.

Confidentially, I am as bitter as the water. Why didn't Jehovah select *me* to lead the people out of Egypt? I wasn't a pretty boy like this Moses — he didn't suffer with us during the trials of building the pyramids. He just showed up and took charge. I am bitter with God *and* with His servant. But no matter — if I have my way I will eventually rule.

Moses came up with some wild idea about cutting down a tree and casting it into the water. It *did* make the water taste sweet, but I had already won the victory. I named the place "Marah," which means "bitter"; the name sticks. Score one point for Gaddi; zero for Moses.

We left Marah and traveled to a nice place named Elim. Elim was an oasis with twelve springs of water and seventy date palms. In my mind we had reached paradise. I thought, "Let's just stay here. This is the life." I laid claim to some waterfront property and pitched my tent

But our bonehead-in-chief, *Moses*, explained that God wanted us to leave. What an idiot! He made my job an easy one.

Have you heard of the concept, "progressive revelation?" Bible scholars have pointed out that God unveiled certain doctrines a little at a time, with the final culmination of various principles found only in the New Testament.

For instance, a chant was popularized during the war in Viet-Nam. Large groups of protestors would assemble and shout the words, "Hell no, we won't go!" We Old Testament folks had never heard of that place; as a result, I started another refrain, "Sheol no, we won't go! Sheol no, we won't go!"

But Moses ignored us. He led us out of Shur and back into the Wilderness.

I had already played the *water* "card." Now it was time for the *food* "card." I asked, "What about food? We have water, but now we are going to starve to death."

Moses apparently hadn't thought about

that one, either. He had to run and ask his God what he should do. While he was talking to the Lord, I was talking to the people. I asked, "Did any of you sign up for *this*?"

"No," they responded. I sneered as I rubbed my hands together. I thought, "It will only be a matter of time. I am going to be the winner."

Moses returned. He said, "Here's the plan. God will give us bread in the morning and meat at night."

"Humph," I thought. "I like meat with my breakfast. And bread will make you fat."

So God sent us quail to eat at night — that's not bad. But the bread He sent us — it was awful. I gave it a name: "manna." And the name, like "Marah," stuck. And it turned out to be a very good name; it meant, "What is it?" You may have also asked your wives the same thing on more than one occasion: "What is it?"

Moses told us to trust God; we were only to gather as much manna as each one of us could eat in a single day. I thought, "Trust God? Isn't He the one that told us to come out here? There is no way!"

So I gathered enough manna for an entire week. The other losers would have to go back out again tomorrow, but not me; I could sleep late.

When I awakened the next afternoon (I am a late sleeper), I reached into my bowl of bread. It was a good thing the sun was already up. I was about to place a handful of manna into my mouth, when *something* fell onto my beard — and it was moving! I threw the bread down and plucked the writhing creature from my face — it was a worm! I looked into the bowl and discovered that the bread was full of them.

I marched straight into Moses' tent with the squirming evidence between my thumb and forefinger. I demanded, "What is this?" Moses laughed. He said, "You apparently didn't listen to my instructions. You were only supposed to gather enough bread for one day. God will give you a fresh supply every day — you can't store it" (Tupperware™ had yet to be invented)

I replied, "Well, you still should have told us about the worms. Is there anything else we should know?"

"Yes Gaddi, there is one more thing. I *did*

tell you this—gather twice as much on Friday so you won't have to work on Saturday. Saturday is our Sabbath: our God-ordained day of rest."

I stormed out of his tent, muttering under my breath. I was certain I was not the only one that had neither listened to, nor obeyed, Moses. I knew what I would do—I would tell my all of my neighbors that the best manna would only be available on Saturdays; that, in my opinion, Moses was trying to keep the good stuff for himself.

So late Friday afternoon I paid a visit to my neighbors' tents. I told them my story. They went out the next morning to gather bread, but there was none to be found. They returned empty-handed. I smiled as I heard other disappointed Israelites grumbling about Moses.

I met individually with my neighbors. "Divide and conquer," I have always said. I asked them, "How long will we allow Moses to dictate how we live our lives? He tells us *what* to eat and *when* to eat and how to gather our food; the next thing you know, he will be telling us where we should go to relieve ourselves." And I was right—he eventually did![24] See what I mean? Talk about micromanaging!

So we suffered through the manna, and we learned to gather it exactly as Moses had instructed us. But I had a lot of time to think. How can I *really* hurt Moses' reputation and turn the people against him?

There is a new saying going around. It may be an *old* saying for you. "When the cat's away, the mice will play." Moses left us for forty days to go up to the top of some mountain to talk with God. I immediately thought, "Party!"

I persuaded Moses' brother Aaron to join with us. It seems that he likes to party, too. We took all of our gold and melted it down. We made a golden calf that looked a lot like the idols we had seen in Egypt. We broke out the wine and started wife-swapping. It was a blast!

And then Moses, that old killjoy, came down off the mountain with two stone tablets in his hands. He threw them on the ground and broke them.

Moses spoke to Aaron for a moment and then walked up to our statue. He treated our calf

---

[24] Deuteronomy 23:12-14.

the same way he had treated his two stone tablets: he cast it onto the ground. The idol shattered. Moses pulverized the golden pieces, poured the powder into our water, and made us drink it. We were all sick! And, if that had not been enough, the Levites drew their swords and killed 3,000 people; it was a massacre! Maybe our celebration wasn't such a good idea after all.

As I said, I had plenty of time to think. I came up with a dastardly plan. Approaching his sister, Miriam, I said, "You've got to do something about Mrs. Moses. You are Moses' older sister, and Aaron is our high priest. If I were the two of you I would walk right up to my brother and tell him what I thought about his 'first lady'."

I watched as Miriam considered my statement. Directly, she rose up from her perch and walked away. I followed her from a distance as she entered Aaron's tent. I laughed to myself, "this is going to be fun. I'm not so sure I want to hold the top spot anymore. If I become the leader, everyone else will be taking shots at me."

Miriam obviously convinced Aaron to

help her as she confronted their brother.[25] "We don't like your wife," she said. Moses looked suspiciously at his older sister. He asked, "Is that your *real* problem? Or is there something else?" She replied, "Since you asked — there *is* something else."

Like Gaddi, I had to give Moses credit. He knew something more important, more significant, was bothering her. As someone has said, "People usually have two reasons for doing something: the one that sounds good and the real reason." So he asked, "What is it, Miriam?"

"I will tell you, Moses," she said. "Why do you think you are God's only spokesperson? I am the one that wrote the song after we crossed the Red Sea. Our brother here," she said as she pointed to Aaron, "is supposed to be your spokesman. You don't have the corner on hearing from God."

I am thankful I let those two do my dirty work for me. The story continues in Numbers 12:9-10: "So the anger of the Lord burned against them and He departed. But when the cloud had withdrawn from over the tent, behold, Miriam

---

[25] Numbers 12:1-2a.

was leprous, as white as snow." And then, "As Aaron turned toward Miriam, behold, she was leprous." I had just experienced two victories: I turned Miriam and Aaron against their brother, and I also helped turn God against Miriam. What a day!

Poor Moses—he was so confused. He didn't seem to know whom he could trust as his friends. For that matter, he didn't know who his real enemies were, either.

My New Testament Counterparts: "I'm back—and I brought friends!"

My New Testament counterparts will include a multitude from the entire Jewish nation. Jesus will perform many miracles for all to see, including raising Lazarus from the dead. Their response will be, "What sign do You show us as your authority for doing these things?"[26] The church leaders, the scribes, and the Pharisees will also say to Him, "Teacher, we want to see a sign

---

[26] John 2:18.

from You."[27]

My favorite, however, will be King Herod. The beloved physician,[28] Luke, will tell you, "Now Herod was very glad when he saw Jesus; for he had wanted to see Him for a long time, because he had been hearing about Him and was hoping to see some sign performed by Him." Jesus, apparently not realizing the gravity of the situation, will remain silent.[29]

Jeff Foxworthy popularized the saying, "You might be a redneck if…" Some examples:[30]

1. You think "loading the dishwasher" means getting your wife drunk.
2. You ever cut your grass and found a car.
3. You own a home that is mobile and five cars that aren't.
4. You think the stock market has a fence

---

[27] Matthew 12:38.
[28] Colossians 4:14.
[29] Luke 23:8-9.
[30]

http://www.countryhumor.com/redneck/mightbe.htm, site visited on 8/25/2011.

around it.

5. Your stereo speakers used to belong to the Drive-in Theater.

6. Your boat has not left the driveway in 15 years.
7. You own a homemade fur coat.
8. Chiggers are included on your list of top five hygiene concerns.
9. You burn your yard rather than mow it.
10. Your wife has ever said, "Come move this transmission so I can take a bath."

To echo this concept, the following quotations have been taken from a blog on Monday, July 30, 2007, entitled "Top Ten Criticisms from a Church and a Response from the Deacon Board (since everyone ran the pastor off)."[31]   There may be a juvenile delinquent in

---

[31] http://churchgrowth1.blogspot.com/2007/07/top-ten-criticisms-from-church-and.html, site visited on 8/25/2011.

your church if someone has ever said:

1. "I want more depth in the sermons."
2. "Nobody noticed when I was gone for three weeks."
3. "Nobody cares about how I feel."
4. "I don't know everybody anymore."
5. "The choir doesn't sing my kind of music."
6. "We shouldn't let those kinds of people into the church."
7. "All the church talks about is for me to give more money."
8. "The preacher talks too much about sacrifice."
9. "The worship services are boring."
10. "The church is not going in the right direction."

And, to round it all out, "you might be the *pastor* of a Wilderness church if…" someone has ever approached you on your way to the pulpit with an empty toilet paper roll, and has demanded that *you* replace it *right now* … in the *ladies'* rest room!

My Epitaph: "I take my ball and go home!"

As a "juvenile delinquent," I have spent my entire Christian life as a spiritual welfare recipient. I have never been satisfied. My expectation level and subsequent demands for Pastor Moses have risen incrementally over time. I have consistently complained about what I didn't like about him. If we had called a new pastor, he likely would have made the mistake of catering to my demands; if he had done so, he would soon have discovered that I would have started compiling a new list of things I didn't like about *him*!

Paul will describe my wasted life in 1 Corinthians 10:1-5:

> *For I do not want you to be unaware, brethren, that our fathers were all under the cloud and all passed through the sea; and all were baptized into Moses in the cloud and in the sea; and all ate the same spiritual food; and all drank the*

same spiritual drink, for they were drinking from a spiritual rock which followed them; and the rock was Christ. Nevertheless, with most of them God was not well-pleased; for they were laid low in the wilderness.

My favorite name for God has been Jehovah-jireh, "the God Who provides." I have always been a consumer. And that has been the extent of my relationship with Him—expecting Him to furnish my every need every day of my miserable life.

Someone has well said that amusement is "to not think." God has not kept me amused; He has never provided *enough*! Yesterday's miracles, like yesterday's manna, have been of no use to me today. He just wouldn't play *my* games according to *my* rules.[32]

My tombstone reads: "Abidan—Common Man—Symbol of the Generation that Refused to Grow Up—Died Spiritually at 40—Buried at 80—

---

[32] Luke 7:31-32.

3 years old."

Abidan

Nevertheless, the crowd and I invite you to
"FOLLOW US!"

THE OVERWHELMED

PASTOR

Hello. My name is Moses. My name means "drawn," a reference to the miraculous story of my birth. I was placed in a basket by my mother and *drawn out* of the river by Pharaoh's daughter. Looking back, she *should* have named me עצם יגע — Yagea 'etsem, which means "the man with the weary bones." I am constantly exhausted!

Someone has well said that I am the pastor of the "First Baptist Church of the Wilderness." I am the chief nursery worker in charge of a nation of spiritual infants. Some days I think I will lose my mind; on other days I *know* I already have! I change this one's diaper and reassure that one; rock this one to sleep and break up that fight—

forever running from one "crisis" to the next.

My Résumé

Why God picked *me*, I will never know. I am the least qualified person to lead anybody to do anything. And He chose me to lead millions of people.

Here is my résumé: basically, a listing of my inadequacies:[33]

- I am fearful
- I am unworthy
- I am ignorant
- I am unconvincing
- I am inarticulate
- I am unwilling

God doesn't seem to understand. I don't want this job! One thing I have discovered over the years, however, is that arguing with God has been somewhat like arguing with my wife,

---

[33] Exodus 3:6-13; 4:1-13.

Zipporah: I always seem to lose.

My Training

I was eighty years old when God first sent
me to speak to Pharaoh? You ask, "Why did He
choose you?" I have asked the same question on
many occasions. But, from God's point-of-view, I
was the most likely candidate.

In Egypt

Pharaoh, the ruler, or king, of Egypt, saw
that the tribes of Israel were quickly
outnumbering his people, the Egyptians. His
plan: to instruct the Hebrew labor and delivery
nurses to kill all the male children at the point of
birth. The midwives, Shiphrah and Puah,
according to Exodus 1:17, "feared god, and did
not do as the king of Egypt had commanded
them, but let the boys live."

Their obedience to God, along with God's
miraculous provision, allowed me to grow up in
Pharaoh's court; I became known as "the son of
Pharaoh's daughter." I received everything that

I, as a person of royalty, could have ever wanted — the best food, the finest clothing, the most luxurious residence, and the most expensive education.

My *spiritual* upbringing, however, was provided by my birth mother. Pharaoh's daughter paid her to take care of me during my infancy. She instilled a fear and a reverence in me for the one true God, Jehovah. She taught me about my heritage as an Israelite.

After forty years, I realized I had a choice to make. I could become either an Egyptian or an Israelite; I couldn't become both.

I had been watching the Egyptians mistreat the Hebrews for weeks. My heart — I would later discover that God had given me a *shepherd's* heart — went out to the Hebrews.[34]

The anger began to well up inside of me. Finally, one day, I exploded. An Egyptian was beating one of my Hebrew brothers. The Hebrew man ran away. I looked around and took note of the fact that the Egyptian was now alone. I grabbed the Egyptian and began to hit him. I didn't stop until he was dead. I buried him so

---

[34] Exodus 2:11-14.

that no one would ever know what I had done —
or so I thought.

Have you noticed that when you do
something wrong, you pretend as if nothing has
happened? As usual, I went out the next morning
to speak to my Hebrew brothers. Everything was
going great, until I saw two Hebrews fighting.
"Break it up, guys," I said.

One of the men looked at me — I mean
really looked at me. He seemed to be gazing into
my very soul. And then he laughed. "Just who
do you think you are?" he asked. "Aren't you an
Egyptian? We have heard that you are the son of
Pharaoh's daughter."

Once again, he took on a more serious
demeanor. He continued, "And besides, aren't
you the man that killed that Egyptian yesterday?
I guess if the two of us don't stop fighting you are
going to kill one of us, too." He looked at the
other man; this time, they *both* laughed.

I thought, "If this guy knows about it, the
whole world will soon know about it. I had better
pack my stuff and leave." And so I did.

I was right to be concerned. Exodus 2:15a
states, "When Pharaoh heard of this matter, he

tried to kill [me]." I willingly surrendered all of my advantages, and fled into the Wilderness.

In the Wilderness

I am continually amazed at God's ability to take something that *seems* to be bad and make something good out of it.[35] Anachronistically, "If the world hands you a lemon, make lemonade." I had no idea that when I fled from Pharaoh that God would use my experiences in the Wilderness to prepare me to become a part of His greater plan. The Lord would take the next forty years to prepare me to become, unbeknownst to me, the guide for His people. I would lead them out of Egypt, across the Wilderness and, hopefully, into the promised land of Canaan.

My next years were spent, or should I say *invested*, in learning how to survive the rigors of the Wilderness. Through events that many would consider as coincidental, I was introduced to my future father-in-law — a man named

---

[35] Genesis 50:20.

Jethro.[36] His name means, "His abundance."

"But Moses," you ask, "how could God use an *unbeliever* to teach you anything? Don't you realize that the Midianites are your enemies? You need to read what *you* wrote under the inspiration of God's Holy Spirit in Genesis 37:26-28":

> *Judah said to his brothers, "What profit is it for us to kill our brother and cover up his blood? Come and let us sell him to the Ishmaelites and not lay our hands on him, for he is our brother, our own flesh." And his brothers listened to him. Then some Midianite traders passed by, so they pulled him up and lifted Joseph out of the pit, and sold him to the Ishmaelites for twenty shekels of silver. Thus they brought Joseph into Egypt.*

You continue, "Moses, don't you see? Midianites are Ishmaelites! Ishmael was the son of a maid named Hagar. Abraham sent him away. There is no love lost between the Israelites and the Ishmaelites. Didn't you also write Genesis 16:10-

---

[36] Exodus 2:16-25.

12?   The preincarnate Christ, speaking with Ishmael's mother, Hagar, said":

> *I will greatly multiply your descendants so that they will be too many to count. Behold, you are with child, and you will bear a son; and you shall call his name Ishmael, because the Lord has given heed to your affliction. He will be a wild donkey of a man, his hand will be against everyone, and everyone's hand will be against him; and he will live to the east of all his brothers.*

I agree with you. It does seem a little outlandish that God would use an Ishmaelite to accomplish His purposes. But my answer to you is twofold: first, the meanest people I have ever met are so-called *believers*; second, God can use *anybody* to do *anything*. Haven't you read the words of Solomon in Proverbs 21:1? He says, "The king's heart is like channels of water in the hand of the Lord; He turns it wherever He wishes."

True   to   his   name,   Jethro   shared   his

abundance with me throughout my Wilderness experience. But he also put me to work. Listen to Exodus 3:1: "Now Moses was pasturing the flock of Jethro his father-in-law, the priest of Midian; and he led the flock to the west side of the wilderness and came to Horeb, the mountain of God."

I became a shepherd. Do you know how Egyptians feel about shepherds? As an Egyptian, I was raised to believe that shepherds and sheep are repulsive, detestable, contemptible, intolerable, disgusting, and nasty. And so they are! And so, quite frankly, are *God's* sheep. Read Joseph's discourse to the members of his family in Genesis 46:33-34:

> *When Pharaoh calls you and says, "What is your occupation?" You shall say, "Your servants have been keepers of livestock from our youth even until now, both we and our fathers," that you may live in the land of Goshen; for every shepherd is* **loathsome** *[emphasis added] to the Egyptians.*

So God has used my work as a shepherd to teach

me humility — a much needed quality in my life as a leader. He has also taught me a lot about human nature — there really isn't much difference between leading sheep and leading Jehovah's people. According to a post on the Central Africa Baptist College website,[37] there are six basic similarities:

1. *Sheep are "clean" animals (Leviticus 11:1-8)*
2. *Sheep are productive animals*
3. *Sheep are safest in the flock.*
4. *Sheep tend to stray*
5. *Sheep need a shepherd*
6. *Sheep know the voice of their shepherd*

Yes, God placed Jethro in my life to "show me the ropes" of dealing both with difficult circumstances and with difficult people. Much of what I have learned about patience, I have learned from him.

I jokingly claim that the only bad thing he

---

[37]

http://www.cabcollege.org/site/user/files/Psalm%2010 0_The%20Sheep%20of%20His %20Pasture.pdf, site visited on 8/30/2011.

has ever given me is his daughter. She was fittingly named Zipporah, which means "bird." Need I say more?

My Audience with Pharaoh

The Lord warned me in Exodus 4:21: "When you go back to Egypt see that you perform before Pharaoh all the wonders which I have put in your power; but I will *harden* his heart so that he will not let the people go." And God was certainly true to His word! Pharaoh's heart became more and more "strengthened, firm, and resolute."[38]

God sent ten plagues through which I issued ten warnings to Pharaoh. He wouldn't listen; he laughed at Aaron and me. His oft repeated message, found in Exodus 5:2 was, "who is the LORD that I should obey his voice to let Israel go? I do not know the LORD, and besides, I will not let Israel go."

Each time, Pharaoh would bargain with

---

[38] R. Laird Harris, Gleason L. Archer, Jr., and Bruce K. Waltke, eds., Theological Wordbook of the Old Testament, (Chicago: Moody Press, 1980).

me to take away the plagues. But then he would renege. He finally allowed us to depart from Egypt when the Death Angel took the life of his firstborn son, along with the lives of all of the firstborn sons of the Egyptians.

The times I spoke with Pharaoh have certainly prepared me for the conflicts I would face in the Wilderness. God's "sheep" can be just as obstinate as any ungodly king.

My Audience with God

How would I describe my relationship with God? I wrote in Exodus 33:11a, "Thus the Lord used to speak to [me] face to face, just as a man speaks to his friend." Imagine that? I am God's friend! I tell Him my thoughts and feelings; I intercede with Him on behalf of His people, and He hears me. He shares His plans with me and He shows His glory to me. And, in contrast with both my initial meeting with Him (when He refused to take "No" for an answer in giving me this "cushy" assignment) and to my henpecked relationship with Zipporah, *God* will *occasionally* allow me to win an argument.[39]

My Ministry

Since God had both called me and commissioned me, I thought that my message would have been accepted. I would soon discover that would not be the case.

I will begin with a high school biology lesson. Perhaps you have learned, as many have, the outdated theory that "ontogeny recapitulates phylogeny?" For those of you that have, this will be a refresher course. For those of you that haven't — you could visit a website created by the University of California Museum of Paleontology.[40] They tell us: "This phrase [ontogeny recapitulates phylogeny] suggests that an organism's development will take it through each of the adult stages of its evolutionary history, or its phylogeny." God rejects that theory; most scientists today would have to agree

---

[39] Exodus 32:7-14.

[40]

http://evolution.berkeley.edu/evosite/evo101/IIIC6aOnt ogeny.shtml, site visited on 8/27/2011.

with Him.

And, because you and I believe that God created the world and everything in it, we would also reject the ontogeny theory. I, Moses, personally dismiss the theory of evolution in its entirety. But who am I?

The ontogeny theory can be useful in giving us a handle on the fact that God's people seem to be going through some continual process. They cry out for a messiah (another name for a deliverer), God sends them one, and they reject him.

God-called pastors and other leaders throughout history will also learn the lesson of rejection. But, if you are a pastor, realize this: you are in good company. God's people will eventually reject *the* Messiah, Jesus Christ, when He comes. So I will become a deliverer and I, too, will be rejected.

I guess I was not surprised when Pharaoh rejected both me and my message. I was, however, stunned to discover that God's own people would systematically reject me! First, I didn't cry out to the Lord to send me to do this job — *they* pleaded with Him to send a deliverer![41]

Second, my own brother turned against me and my leadership when I was on the mountain receiving the Ten Commandments from God.

Third, the Israelites refused to go into the Promised Land when I had led them there and had instructed them to do so.

Fourth, they decided to call a new pastor — one that would lead them *back* to Egypt! Only the Lord's intervention prevented them from "terminating" Aaron, Caleb, Joshua, and me — with rocks!

Fifth, they attempted to go into the Promised Land after the Lord had closed the door. I clearly instructed them to refrain from this action.[42]

Sixth, the weeks and months of complaining against my leadership finally culminated in a showdown initiated by a family of Levites known as the Korahites.

Seventh, the Israelites complained about the lack of water — again. Only this time, it was

---

[41] Exodus 2:23-25.
[42] Numbers 14:39-45.

immediately after the death of my sister, Miriam.

Eighth, the people never learned to stop complaining. Numbers 21:4c says, "And the people became impatient because of the journey." Continuing the thought in verse five, "The people spoke against God and Moses." They said, "Why have you brought us up out of Egypt to die in the Wilderness? For there is no food and no water, and we loathe this miserable food." As a result, "The Lord sent fiery serpents among the people and they bit the people, so that many people of Israel died."[43]

Ninth, the juvenile delinquents, against the clear command from God that I had declared to them, intermarried with the Moabites.[44] In response, God sent a plague that killed 24,000 people.[45] But it didn't matter; they were already destined to die in the Wilderness. They simply

[43] Numbers 21:6.
[44] Exodus 34:11-16.
[45] Numbers 25.

accelerated the process.

My Fatigue

I am tired. Two events that occurred early in our Wilderness journey demonstrated my weariness. First, the people had just finished whining and complaining about not having water. I struck the rock; God provided more than enough for us all. I then received word that the Amalekites, like cur dogs, were nipping at the heels of my people — *God's* people.[46]

I was irate! I thought back about my experience in Egypt. You remember: when I killed the Egyptian and buried him in the sand. I thought about circling around and catching some of them unawares. But then I realized something: I was simply too tired to fight.

As a shepherd I called my "sheep dog," Joshua, to my side. I thought, "He will protect the sheep." I then told him to select a group of

---

[46] Deuteronomy 25:17-18.

warriors and prepare to fight.

I did my part. I climbed to the top of the hill overlooking Rephidim.[47] Interestingly, the name Rephidim means "resting places." I held the rod of God in the air. The battle went in our favor. But as I grew weary and my arms fell to my sides, we retreated.

Aaron and Hur to the rescue! They carried large rock for me to sit on, and reached up to hold up my hands. I realized, for the first time, that I couldn't do it all. And so I rested. I had found my *Rephidim*.

The second event that illustrated my exhaustion occurred when Jethro, my father-in-law, brought my wife, Zipporah, and two sons back to me.[48] Why had they left me? It's a long story but, during my time in the Wilderness, I had begun to neglect my relationship with Jehovah God. I couldn't really blame anyone other than myself. But, at that particular point in time, Jethro's household, including my wife, didn't worship my God.

As you know, God had made a covenant

---

[47] Exodus 17:8-13.
[48] Exodus 4:24-26.

with my ancestor, Abraham. The sign of the covenant was the circumcision of every male child eight days after their births.[49] I should have told Zipporah what I was about to do, but I didn't. I said, "I will watch baby Gershom for a little while. You go and get some rest." She smiled as she walked away; she must have been thinking, "What a thoughtful husband." I knew differently.

I placed our son on the kitchen table, picked up a sharp knife, and transformed him into a good Israelite. Zipporah heard the screams and came running. When she saw the blood, she shrieked. She gave me a look that I will never forget—let me just say that it wasn't pleasant.

As a result of that experience I decided that, in order to keep peace at home, I would refrain from circumcising our youngest son, Eliezer. Not that I *could* have circumcised him. Zipporah planted herself firmly between us and watched over him, like a hawk, day and night for months!

Years later, I was returning to Egypt with my wife and two sons. I was obeying God's

---

[49] Genesis 17:10-13.

calling for me to speak to Pharaoh—or so I thought.

I became very sick as I thought of my future meetings with Pharaoh. When Zipporah asked what was wrong with me I said, "I am going to die because of my disobedience to God." She asked, "Disobedience—what are you talking about?" I proceeded to explain to her the sign of God's covenant with Abraham; my illness was the result of the fact that our son, Eliezer, had not been circumcised.

She reached down to the ground and picked up a flint rock. She grabbed Eliezer, kicking and screaming, and performed the ritual right there in front of me. She threw his bloody foreskin at my feet. She asked, "Is *your* God satisfied now, Moses?" Needless to say, the two of us needed some alone time! She took our kids and went home to daddy.

I assume Jethro had spoken with her about the situation. He apparently felt the time was right for us to be reunited. He watched me from a distance for several hours. He finally walked up to me. I was in the middle of a meeting with some of the Hebrews when he interrupted with, "What in the world are you doing?"[50]

"What do you mean?" I sheepishly responded. He continued, "I have been observing you all day long. One group of people comes to you with their complaints or concerns; you listen to them, and then tell them what they should do. As soon as they leave, more people approach you. It never ends. I had to take a number and wait. Son, you can't keep this up forever — it will wear you out!"

I nodded in agreement. "You're right, Dad. But I'm the *pastor*; it's my *job*."

He grabbed my shoulders and looked me squarely in the eyes. "No, son, it's not. One man cannot possibly do what you are attempting to do. It will *kill* you. And then they won't have a pastor at all, will they?" I protested, "But *they* expect it — *God* expects it."

"No, He doesn't, Moses," Jethro replied. "I have an idea — you take care of the preaching and the praying; let some other guys assist you with the pastoral responsibilities. They could handle the low-level squabbles, and bring the big stuff to

---

[50] Exodus 18:13-27.

you."

I thought, "That is a great idea!" In fact, it was such a good idea that the New Testament apostles will one day follow suit.[51] I selected 70 men to help me; Jethro went home.

Have you ever noticed that everything works great—in *theory*? The people would visit with their appointed representatives just long enough to say the problem was too big to be solved by some low-level flunkies. "We want to see the big guy," they would demand. And so my days were spent—once again—listening to the complaints, large and small, of literally millions of people.

You modern day pastors should have no difficulty in understanding my dilemma. One of your teachers, deacons, or elders may be allowed to visit a sick church member. But your members will always expect you, their *pastor*, to come and see them—*regardless* of the size of your church. And you had better do it, because you are the only *employee* some of your church members will ever have!

One day I was complaining about my

---

[51] Acts 6:1-4.

circumstances to the Lord. He told me the problem with Jethro's idea was that I had forgotten to involve *Him*—the Lord—in the process. I asked, "What should I do? How should I have done it?"

God replied, "You need to have a special service—an ordination service—during which the people will see that My hand is also upon these men." So we had our service.[52] God visibly came down for all to see. The 70 prophesied and, for the first time, the people began to recognize their God-given authority. Once they saw the evidence of God's working in the lives of the elders, they allowed these men to deal with their mundane, day-to-day concerns.[53]

Looking back, I now think to myself, "Why didn't we do it this way a long time ago? Maybe even *forty* years ago?"

Note to future pastors: the people won't follow a man with the position of elder until *after* he has given clear evidence of God's power in his life! Do you remember David's "mighty men?"[54]

---

[52] Numbers 11:24-30.
[53] Acts 6:3.
[54] 1 Chronicles 11:10-47.

They were promoted to their positions *after* they had experienced success in battle. And don't forget Othniel. He was handpicked to be Caleb's son-in-law only *after* he had proved himself in combat.[55]

You pastors will be tempted to promote people that have either no track record at all or a poor one. And then you will hope these folks will somehow measure up. How is that working out for you?

Note to future deacons: the office of a deacon is clearly distinct from the office of an elder. As a deacon, you are *not* an elder.[56]

My Disobedience

I *almost* made it. I *almost* listened to God. I *almost* obeyed His voice. Unfortunately, the only time that *almost* counts is in a game you will one day call "horseshoes."

Miriam had long since fallen out of favor with the people. She had confronted me and, as a result, contracted leprosy. The people despised

---

[55] Judges 1:12-13.
[56] 1 Timothy 3:1-16; Titus 1:6-16.

her for making them tarry until she could rejoin us as we resumed our journey. I thought, "What is the hurry? We are not really going anywhere. We are just wandering around in circles. Where do you people think that you need to be?"

They had forgotten the song of God's deliverance she had taught them; they had disregarded her part in saving my life and delivering me into the safekeeping of Pharaoh's daughter. But I hadn't forgotten. I loved her although, I have to admit, she and I had not been very close since the "leprosy incident."

And then, one day, she fell dead along the path. No one stopped to check her condition. No one offered to help. They just stepped over, or around, her now lifeless body. One man even stepped *on* her! Aaron and I had to pick her up and bury her! No one else even attended her funeral. I preached; Aaron listened. Either no one seemed to notice the grief on my face or they just didn't care.

I was deeply wounded by their indifference. And my pain turned into anger. I wish I had understood what you believers will one day take for granted. Jesus' half-brother will write in James 1:19-20: "This you know, my beloved brethren. But everyone must be quick to hear, slow to speak and slow to anger; for the anger of man does not achieve the righteousness of God."

I intellectually justified my disobedience to the Lord. I thought, "He will surely understand my actions." But I was out of control; I was out of *His* control. For the first time in forty years, I had grown to hate the children of Israel.

I want you to imagine that I am playing in a major tournament of the game you will one day call "golf." I am on the eighteenth hole, three strokes ahead of my nearest competitor, and only one inch from the cup.

I take the putter from my bag and then look down at the ball. I see Gaddi's face emblazoned upon it! I return my putter and take out my driver and a tee. I jerk the ball, along with a fistful of grass, from the ground and place it on the tee. My jaw is clenched as I take my swing. Everyone is horrified. All eyes are upon me as I hit the ball so hard that it goes completely off of the course, shattering a window in the clubhouse.

Would you say that, as a golfer, I would

have been disqualified? Of course! And, as a leader, I will also be disqualified. God spoke to Aaron and me in Numbers 20:12: "Because you have not believed Me, to treat Me as holy in the sight of the sons of Israel, therefore you shall not bring this assembly into the land which I have given them."

My Epitaph

I praise the Lord for His grace and His mercy. Even though He didn't allow me to *physically* enter the Promised Land, He did allow me to *see* it.

Just before I died, God summoned me to the highest point of Mount Nebo — a place known as Pisgah, or "cleft" — reminiscent of the place where He had previously revealed His glory to me in Exodus 33. According to Deuteronomy 34:1b-4:

> *The Lord showed [me] all the land, Gilead as far as Dan, and all Naphtali and the land of Ephraim and Manasseh, and all the land of Judah as far as the western sea, and the Negev*

and the plain in the valley of Jericho, the city of palm trees, as far as Zoar. Then the Lord said to [me], "This is the land which I swore to Abraham, Isaac, and Jacob, saying, 'I will give it to your descendants;' I have let you see it with your eyes, but you shall not go over there."

My death is described in verses 5-8:

So [I] died there in the land of Moab, according to the word of the Lord. And He buried [me] in the valley in the land of Moab, opposite Beth-peor; but no man knows [my] burial place to this day. Although [I] was one hundred and twenty years old when [I] died, [my] eye was not dim, nor [my] vigor abated.

I wish I could have been present at my memorial service. The people wept over me for thirty days! It seems that people never really appreciate us until long after we are gone.

I have tried my best to be a peacemaker. My favorite name for God, therefore, has been

Jehovah-shalom, which means, "God is peace."

If I had been given a tombstone, I would have wanted it to read: "Moses — servant of the Lord."[57] Perhaps the best tribute I have ever received is found in Deuteronomy 34:10-12:

> *Since that time no prophet has risen in Israel like Moses, whom the Lord knew face to face, for all the signs and wonders which the Lord sent him to perform in the land of Egypt against Pharaoh, all his servants, and all his land, and for all the mighty power and for all the great terror which Moses performed in the sight of all Israel.*

I was never given a grave marker, and I didn't have the opportunity to lead the Israelites into the Promised Land. But don't cry for me. I am in the *Heavenly* Promised Land. I am now beholding God's glory — something I had always desired to do on the Earth. I could never experience it while I was trapped in human flesh.

---

[57] Exodus 14:30-31.

When God sets you free, you are free indeed![58]

I hope you will **NOT** "FOLLOW ME!"
(at least not in my acts of disobedience)

THE UNWILLING

IMMIGRANT

You may simply call me "ben-Nemuel," or the son of Nemuel. My name means "the son of the day of God." That's not bad. A better name for me, however, would have been, מהה — maw-hah', which means "the one who lingers, tarries, waits, or delays."

My father had two brothers, Dathan and Abiram. He was the oldest son of Eliab. I am sure you have heard of Dathan. He was nicknamed, "the Radical Nonconformist." Dathan (chapter two) coaxed his younger brother, Abiram, to join with him in a plot to rebel against Moses. He also tried to get my father involved in his conspiracy but, thankfully for me and my family, he failed in that endeavor.

My Résumé

My personal résumé, for your consideration, is as follows:

- I am a nephew of Dathan and Abiram.
- I am a member of the tribe of Reuben.
- I am a great family man. I have sheltered my wife and children from the dangers of Canaan.
- I have helped to build several cities including Heshbon, Elealeh, Kiriathaim, Nebo, Baal-meon, and Sibmah.
- I am a valiant warrior; I led many of the troops into Canaan.

Let's Make a Deal

After all that I have seen during my Wilderness wanderings, I have made a decision: I will *not* go into the Promised Land. I know it is probably a wonderful place, but I have heard there are many dangers there. I have always feared the unknown, and now more than ever.

You ask, "Why are you so fearful?" My reason: I can still remember the looks on the faces of my cousins as they plunged into that abyss. And their screams were bone chilling! Moses warned us to distance ourselves from my cousins. I took his advice; I ran as far away and as quickly as I could. Weeks later, when I finally returned home, I discovered that an additional 15,000 people had died of a plague.

Note to self: "Don't mess with Moses." Second note to self: "Stay right here on *this* side of 'the River' — where it is safe."

My job was to rally the troops — to find others that were also unwilling to cross over. My own tribe members, the Reubenites, quickly agreed with me.

I approached the members of the tribe of Judah. That was a big mistake! I was talking to one of my Judahite friends when the old guy walked up: Caleb. He let me know, with a not-so-friendly shove, that I was wasting my time with his family.

I asked myself, "Is there another tribe that may not be as 'Moses-friendly?' Oh, yes: the tribe of Gad. They haven't fared well since Gaddi, the 'Evil Talebearer,' misled us forty years earlier." Not only that, according to Numbers 32:1a, they had something in common with us Reubenites: "Now the sons of Reuben and the sons of Gad had an exceedingly large number of livestock." And we would have more room to spread out on this side of "the River." The Gadites quickly agreed.

I assembled the Reubenites and the Gadites and made assignments. We worked together to canvass the members of the other tribes. Simeon, Issachar, Zebulun, Benjamin, Dan, Naphtali, Asher, and Ephraim all declined. And get this — half of the tribe of Manasseh also refused; the other half decided to get on board with us.

The Discussion

We have an old saying — even in my time: "There is strength in numbers." Every man, woman, boy, girl, sheep, and cow from the two and one half tribes joined with me as we approached Moses' tent en masse. He asked, "What is this all about?" As the spokesman, I replied, "Moses, we like the land on *this* side of 'the River' — it is perfect for our cattle and sheep. We would like to stay right here." He asked, "Why?" I continued, "Don't you remember the problems that Abram and Lot experienced when they tried to combine their enormous herds on one plot of land? I have the solution — you can send all of the others across; *this* side of 'the River' will become our home."

Moses was obviously displeased with my request.[59] His concerns were basically twofold. He said, 1) "If I allow you to remain on this side of Jordan you will discourage the other Israelites from entering into the Promised Land; 2) you will incite God to anger — everyone (*except* Caleb and Joshua), including the youngsters, will die in the Wilderness."

I quickly nodded in agreement. I knew that Moses wanted to be both heard and understood. I moved a little closer in order to speak confidentially with him.[60] "Listen to me, Moses," I said, "I tell you what: if you will let us stay on *this* side, our men will lead the way into

---

[59] Numbers 32:6b-15.
[60] Numbers 32:16b-19.

the battle on the *other* side. We will fight until the entire land of Canaan has been conquered. And we will release any claim we might have in the Promised Land. *Our* inheritance will be right here."

Moses agreed to my terms with one caveat: "You had better do everything exactly as you have promised, OR." His voice trailed. "Or," I asked. "Or," he continued, "you won't just be breaking your promise to me—you will be sinning against the Lord." And then he made a very terrifying statement—one that you may have heard quoted at one time or another. He said, "Be sure your sin will find you out."[61]

I was not exactly sure about the meaning of that admonition, but I certainly didn't want to find out! "Okay, Moses, we have a deal. We will leave our families on this side of 'the River.' We will cross over and lead our brothers in the fight

---

[61] Numbers 32:23.

for the Lord and for Israel."

The Contract

One of the many lawyers that chase camel drivers through the Wilderness agreed to draw up the contract. The witnesses to our agreement included Eleazar, the priest, Joshua, the son of Nun, and "the heads of the fathers' households of the tribes of the sons of Israel." The contract read as follows:[62]

> *Reuben, Gad, and Manasseh hereby promise to help defeat the enemies of Israel in the land, henceforth referred to as "Canaan." Joshua, et al, will bequeath to the aforementioned Reuben, Gad, and Manasseh the land on the west side of "the River," henceforth referred to as "Gilead," for their inheritance.*
>
> *Failing to meet the aforementioned conditions, Reuben and company will forfeit all claims to "Gilead." They will consequently receive their allotted portions with the other Israelites in*

---

[62] Numbers 32:28-32.

"Canaan."

Attested to by our signatures this, the fifth day of Nisan in the year *before* the coming of our Messiah, the Lord Jesus Christ, fourteen hundred and six.

Signed: נמואלבן־ (ben-Nemuel)

השמ (Moses)

Witnesses: והישעו (Joshua)

אלעזר (Eleazar)

My Blunder

I would like to say that everything went well from that point on, but it didn't. We *did* lead the other tribes into battle. We *did* keep our side of the bargain. But when we returned to our side of "the River," we made a nearly fatal mistake: we built a large altar by the riverside on *their* side of "the River."

Members of the tribes on the Canaan side of "the River" had already indicated they didn't much care for us. They really didn't agree with the arrangement we had made with Moses.

I have to admit that we probably should have built the altar on *our* side of "the River." Erecting a memorial on *their* side may have been a bad idea. We saw the seasoned warriors on the other side as they were preparing for battle — with *us*!

Thank the Lord that reason (and our prayers) prevailed. They assembled a delegation consisting of eleven men. According to Joshua 22:13b-14:

> *Phinehas the son of Eleazar the priest, and with him ten chiefs, one chief for each father's household from each of the tribes of Israel; and each one of them was the head of his father's household among the thousands of Israel.*

Phineas, the spokesman, approached me. He asked, "What were you guys thinking? You are obviously rebelling against God. Don't you remember the last time we disobeyed God? He was so angry with us that He sent a plague that killed 24,000 people! Do you really want to stir Him up again? Listen! If you don't like it over here, we will be more than happy to let you join us over *there*," he said, as he pointed across "the River."   As an afterthought, and for good measure, Phineas also included his explanation of the sins of Achan and his resultant judgment from God.[63]

I have always prided myself in my ability to "think on my feet." I responded, "It's not like that, Phineas. The Lord knows our hearts. We didn't build that altar as an act of rebellion; we placed it there as a reminder to future generations on both sides of 'the River' that we, too, are the sons of Israel. We will always be your brothers. We want to avoid war with you, both now *and* in the future."

Phineas smiled. I had won him over. He replied, in Joshua 22:31b, "Today we know that the Lord is in our midst, because you have not committed this unfaithful act against the Lord; now you have delivered the sons of Israel from the hand of the Lord."

He and the ten men returned to Canaan. We anachronistically watched through our binoculars as Phineas related my response. The

---

[63] Joshua 7:16-25.

people appeared to be happy as they waved to us. Phineas led them in prayer, thanking the Lord for preventing them from waging a war with us. They all turned and marched eastward until they had disappeared from our sight.

Remember the anachronism, "If the world hands you a lemon, make lemonade?" We transformed the situation by calling the altar we had constructed "Witness." We named it that "because," we said, "it is a witness between us that the Lord is God."[64]

My Epitaph

I have never regretted the choices I have made. I have lived a very satisfying life. I have experienced the thrill of battle. I have also effectively protected both my family and my possessions.

After returning home, I lived out the rest of my life on the west side of the Jordan River. I pitched my hammock between two sturdy cacti. I spent many hours there reflecting upon my many wonderful decisions. And then, one day, I

---

[64] Joshua 22:34.

quietly breathed my last.

My tombstone reads: "ben-Nadab — Husband — Family   Man — Spokesman — Warrior — Peacemaker."   I would like to say, "I couldn't have said it better myself," but I can't. I *did* say it myself. I dictated the inscription to my wife *before* I departed.

ben-
Nadab

Oh, and by the way — I heartily invite you to
"FOLLOW ME!"

THE LONE RANGER

I, your humble servant, will become another one of your potential guides as you travel through this seemingly dark period in your life. Let me introduce myself. My name is Caleb, which means "dog." As you will soon discover, a better name for me would have been בד — bad, which means "the one who is alone, by himself, besides, apart, separate, alone." This name comes from a root word, בדד–baw-dad', which means "to withdraw, be separate, be isolated."

I don't have a last name. "Strange," you say? It may be peculiar to you, but not to an Israelite. We are identified by relationships rather than by surnames. You aren't comfortable with that? Then you may call me Caleb ben-Jephunneh or, rather, Caleb the son of Jephunneh.[65]

Moses is going to select twelve of us to

---

[65] Numbers 13:6.

explore Canaan — the Land of Promise; the land God is giving to His people. Moses will commission only one man from each of the twelve tribes of Israel.

I would certainly like to go, but the odds are against me. I am only one warrior out of 75,000 from the tribe of Judah![66] That means, mathematically, that I have a .001% chance of being selected. What a bummer! Why couldn't I have come from the tribe of Manasseh? There are only 32,200 of them.[67]

Joshua, however, is a shoo-in. He is from the tribe of Ephraim, a mid-sized family with 40,500 warriors. But he and Moses have a special relationship. He will later become known as "Moses' servant." If I can't go personally, at least I can go vicariously through Joshua. He will tell me everything when he returns. And then I will be able to see it for myself when we all cross "the River" together in just a few short weeks — forty

---

[66] Numbers 1:27.
[67] Numbers 1:35.

days, to be exact.

My Résumé

My personal résumé, for your consideration, is as follows:

- I am a proud member of the tribe of Judah.
- The name Judah means "praise."
- My mother was a Kenizzite, one of the original tribes of people living in Canaan at the time when God originally promised the land to Abraham. So you could actually say that I am going home.[68]
- I will be one of twelve scouts commissioned by Moses to investigate the Promised Land.
- I will be one of only two spies that will bring back a good report.
- I will be one of only two members of the original group that left Egypt that will be

---

[68] Genesis 15:19.

allowed to live in the Promised Land.

My Version of "The Assignment"

Moses has surely spent a lot of time in prayer! I don't guess I could blame him — he was in charge of transporting millions of us from Egypt to Canaan.

The big day finally arrived. We would find out which ones of us would be selected by Moses. Twelve "lucky" men would be chosen to become spies on assignment to the land of promise known as "Canaan."

I haven't heard of fictional spies like James Bond or real-life spies like Mata Hari. I'm not really sure what spies are supposed to do. "But," I thought, "no matter. I probably won't be picked anyway."

Moses gathered all of the men together. He explained that God Himself had already chosen the twelve spies.

I thought to myself, "Does God even know

who I am? I mean, with so many men in Israel, would he even notice me?"[69]

Moses looked at the warriors from the tribe of Reuben. He called out a name: "Shammua. Shammua ben-Zaccur." A young man ran excitedly to stand by Moses' side. I thought, "He doesn't look so tough. Why would Moses want *him*?"

Moses looked down at his clipboard as he pointed to the representatives from the tribe of Simeon. "Shaphat," he shouted, "son of Hori." "Shaphat," I mused, "that wimp? He once tried to pick a fight with me—I don't believe he will ever try *that* again!"

God's man then faced *my* tribe—the tribe of Judah. He looked around at my cousins. I must admit that many of them were older, or wiser, or stronger than I. My hopes began to sink. With tears in my eyes, I turned to walk away. I began to run. I couldn't stand the thought that someone else might be allowed to go.

I had nearly reached the outskirts of my family gathering, when a voice boomed out.

---

[69] Psalm 8:3-4.

Moses proclaimed, "Caleb, son of Jephunneh." I stopped immediately; I turned around. Not seeing anyone approach, Moses repeated himself. "Is Caleb ben-Jephunneh here?" I shouted, "Yes Moses," as I breathlessly joined the other two men by his side. I didn't hear the names of the other nine men, except one: Joshua (Joshua was known to most of us as Hoshea).[70] Moses thanked everyone for coming, and then met with us briefly to give us our directions.

After we dismissed, Joshua came over to congratulate me. "I'm glad you're on the team with us, Caleb." I responded, "I am too, Joshua. I have dreamed about this day ever since Moses first announced the mission. Can you imagine? The two of us are going to be *spies*!" And then I asked Joshua, "What, exactly, do you think that means?"

Joshua shook his head. "I'm not sure. But I think it involves an all-expense paid vacation into Canaan. I *do* know this: it *has* to be better than living in Egypt! I have never worked so hard in all of my life. I thought I was going to die!"

I nodded in agreement. "You're right

---

[70] Numbers 13:16.

about that! And I know it will be better than *this* place — this Wilderness — this dry, desert land. I can't imagine staying here another night. The sooner we move into our new country, the better."

"I *know* that's right," Joshua said.

The Training

Moses met with the twelve of us. He gave us our instructions:[71]

> *As you are traveling through Canaan, start with the southern part of the land – the Negev. Then check out the hill country. I want you to examine and describe the demographics, the agricultural practices, and the terrain. It should take you approximately forty days; then bring back your report.*

Joshua and I were feverishly taking notes. The other ten guys were whispering among themselves. And laughing!

Moses dismissed us; Joshua and I

---

[71] Numbers 13:17-20.

continued to talk. I asked, "What's wrong with those guys?"

"I don't know, Caleb," Joshua responded. "I don't think they are taking the mission very seriously. And you can't blame them. All we have to do is cross 'the River,' walk around *our* land — the land God has *already* given us — and come back here with our report."

"I guess you're right, Joshua," I said. "But I still don't like it."

He continued, "Stop being a 'Caleb.'" I asked, "What is that supposed to mean?" Joshua said, "You and I both know your name means, 'Dog.' You are just like a dog: always looking for a fight. And once you 'bite into' something you will never let it go."

"Oh, yeah," I said jokingly. And then I grabbed Joshua and wrestled him to the ground. We collapsed there in the dirt; we laughed. "This is going to be great," I thought. I looked over at him and said, "Hey, Joshua, too bad the two of us can't go into Canaan and leave these other guys behind." He nodded in agreement.

I had a bad feeling about the others. You may have heard the term, 'I'm a poet and don't know it.' I will soon discover that, in this particular instance, I am a prophet even though I had never previously prophesied.

The Tour

The twelve of us found a low place in "the River" where we could safely cross. We entered into the Promised Land. We didn't discover much about the flora and fauna in the first few days, but we discovered something about ourselves. The rift between us was beginning to widen.

I would soon discover the reason for our differences. Have you ever noticed that some people like to take pictures of scenery while others prefer to take pictures of people? It was as if the twelve of us were traveling to different places — seeing everything through totally different sets of eyes. Joshua and I were looking through the eyes of faith at the panorama that opened up before us; the other ten were looking through the eyes of fear at size of the inhabitants. *Our* focus was upon the promises of God and what He had already done and what He would do; *their* focus was upon the limitations of humanity—what they had personally done and what they could personally do. I thought to myself, "How sad."

The country was so large that it did, indeed, take us forty days just to walk across it! You may have heard about the argument that took place between a farmer from Texas and a farmer from Arkansas. They both believed their farms were larger than the other's. Finally, the farmer from Texas said, "My farm is so big it takes me all day to drive across it in my truck." Not to be outdone, the farmer from Arkansas replied, "I used to have a truck like that!"

We certainly didn't have time to go everywhere and look at everything, but we saw enough. "What a beautiful place," I thought as I looked around. "And all of us, along with all of our family members, will be coming back in a few days to claim our inheritance. No wonder people call Him, 'Jehovah-jireh.' He truly is 'the God Who provides.' This is more breathtaking than Goshen, even though it was undeniably the best land in all of Egypt. And what about that mountain I can see over there? Maybe one day I can live up there."

The other ten guys didn't seem quite so excited. They stared at Joshua and me as we both laughed excitedly. They, on the other hand, were scowling and murmuring. I looked directly at Igal from the tribe of Issachar. I demanded, "What is your problem?" He just stared back at me with a look of utter disgust.

I looked away from him. I asked another spy, "What about you, Palti? You are from good stock: the tribe of Benjamin. What's bothering you?"

Palti replied, "It's your *attitude*, Caleb." He pointed first at Joshua, and then at me, as he said, "We can't stand the way the two of you seem to be laughing all of the time." I interrupted, "You think Caleb and I have been laughing? You and these other nine losers are the giggle sisters."

He continued, "Don't you realize the importance of this mission? People's lives are at stake — our families will be in danger if we bring them to this God-forsaken place!"

Joshua saw the look in my eyes. He watched as the blood rushed into my face. He noticed my fists clenching and my jaw tightening. He knew what was about to happen—he had seen it many times before. He began to speak loudly enough so that all could hear, "Caleb, everything is okay. They are entitled to their opinion."

He took me aside and quietly said, "Don't worry—we have two advantages." I demanded, "Advantages?" He replied, "Yes, of course! Moses is our leader; he will make the final decision. And God has already told him that the land is ours." I replied, "You're right, Joshua." I stared back at the other ten men. Five of the "giggle sisters" looked relieved; the other five looked ready for a fight. I thought, "Five against one. Those seem like fair odds. In fact, they might be stacked slightly in *my* favor."

The fight, sadly, would have to wait for another day.

The Minority Report

No one could believe the size of the clusters of grapes, pomegranates, and figs Joshua and I brought back with us. The grapes were so large that Joshua and I had to carry them on a pole that we had perched precariously on our right shoulders. The other ten men were, not surprisingly, empty-handed. The people saw two smiling faces and ten somber faces.

Gaddi and the others spoke first. The people were disheartened. I could not stand there quietly—I *had* to speak. I gained the people's attention long enough to utter one sentence: "We should by all means go up and take possession of it, for we will surely overcome it."[72]

Gaddi totally neutralized my statement by his rejoinder. He said:[73]

> *I, for one, am not going back across "the River." You have all marveled at the size of the grapes. Everything over there is huge, especially the people. It would take ten of us to equal one of the towering warriors over there. Caleb and Joshua believe that Canaan is a great place. It would, indeed, be a great place — to*

---

[72] Numbers 13:30.
[73] Numbers 13:31-33.

die!

The other members of "the ten" nodded dutifully in agreement. I glared directly at Gaddi. He didn't finish his statement, so I mentally finished it for him. His blasphemous thoughts were screaming, "People, you must realize that either God was wrong or we misunderstood Him. Even *He* wouldn't be able to handle those giants!"

I stared at Joshua. He returned my gaze with "the look." I know "the look" all too well. He knew exactly what I was preparing to do.

I looked away from Joshua. I fixed my eyes upon Moses. He said nothing. Truly he must have been the meekest and most humble man that has ever lived.[74]

Why didn't someone else say it? I physically turned to look back at Joshua. I could imagine him addressing the crowd with these words: "Men, it *is* true that there are giants in the land. But Jehovah God is on *our* side. Don't you remember what He did to Pharaoh and his army? Have you forgotten the words to the song that

---

[74] Numbers 12:3.

Miriam taught us? Don't listen to Gaddi and these other failures. God says, '*Go,*' so let's go!"

But Joshua remained silent. My heart nearly stopped beating. I was surrounded by a nation of unbelievers! God told us to go in and claim the land, but it was becoming apparent that we wouldn't.

I was selected by Moses because I have always been a leader. I was accustomed to having people listen to me and follow my directions. This time I was ignored. I would much rather have experienced a full frontal assault. Gaddi and the other members of "the ten" simply disregarded me. And, other than Moses and Joshua, everyone else ostracized me. It was as if I did not even exist.

The people retired to their tents to cry all night and to commiserate. My wife looked pleadingly at me as she said, "Caleb, you know how you are. You love to fight. You even think you can be victorious. But you are greatly outnumbered. You need to be *reasonable.*"

"*Reasonable,*" I shouted. "You must be joking! I am operating by something that is much higher than reason—it's a thing called 'faith', something that you and these others are apparently lacking."

Then she gave *me* "the look." I would pay dearly for my comment. We would be eating leftover ba-manna bread for weeks.

Ten Lessons I Have Learned from the Wilderness

I have learned several lessons throughout my journey through the Wilderness. I have not primarily been a thinker. I have always been a man of action. Forgive me, then, that I have not taken the time to list them in any particular order. And I am sure I have left many off. You, my dear reader, have my permission to add to the list.

Lesson One: you come out exactly as you go in

I know my wording may seem strange. Let me explain. Joshua and I went into the Wilderness with a vision. We not only saw the Promised Land—we were, for all intents and purposes, *already* there.

The other ten spies, even though they had physically seen the Promised Land, did not really see it. They may have seen it with their *physical* eyes, but their *spiritual* eyes were closed tightly shut. They missed it. No one else among our contemporaries, except Moses at the end of his life, ever saw the place that God had prepared for us.

Joshua and I maintained our heavenly vision for forty years. We knew that, no matter how long it might take, we would one day live in the land of promise. The others, because of unbelief, would refuse to go there; they were, for all intents and purposes, already dead. Joshua and I would live through our Wilderness experience; everyone else would die in theirs.

So, my dear reader, since you must go through the Wilderness you will have a choice to make. You must ask yourself, "Will I, by faith, carry my vision of the Promised Land with me, or will I die in the Wilderness?" The choice is yours alone to make.

Lesson Two: most people will be defeated by the Wilderness

The Lord never intended for the Wilderness to be a place of conflict and strife. And yet, many people insist on transforming it into just that.

It is true that the Israelites complained about virtually everything in the Wilderness — *no* water or *bitter* water; they didn't like the manna that God provided each day or the double portion before the Sabbath. I could go on and on; my fellow sojourners *did* go on and on!

Even Moses himself was eventually defeated by the Wilderness. You remember the story — *his* story.

For Moses' offense, he would not be allowed to enter in with us into the Land of Promise. I know we should never question the Lord, but that consequence seemed a little harsh. I know God gives grace where grace is needed, but I'm not sure how *I* would have responded if I had been in Moses' sandals.

Lesson Three: what doesn't kill you will make you stronger

Life in the Wilderness can be extremely difficult. Discounting the environmental conditions, the loneliness can often become unbearable. I have discovered that it is possible to be surrounded by millions of people (and their livestock) and still feel like you are all alone. After a period of time, the faces of even your closest friends and relatives begin to swirl into a cloud of nothingness. You look at your own brother and say to yourself, "I think I might know that guy."

The never-ending sameness can sometimes drive you crazy. You get up in the morning asking the question, "What day is it?" It is just like retirement! You respond to your own question with, "What's the difference? One day is the same as the rest. Other than the Sabbath, the day when we worship the Lord, all the other days are identical. We get up, march a few miles in no particular direction, eat, and go to bed."

You ask, "What about the humor in the

Wilderness?" We have become a prison full of lifers that stopped telling the joke and just assigned numbers to them. One inmate would call out the number, everyone would think about the associated witticism, and the entire region would be filled with laughter.

Every conversation is stale! I want to scream when a man asks me if I noticed something unusual about the hill to the left, or when one woman is shocked at what another woman is wearing. I have news for you: we are all wearing the same outfits—right down to the sandals—we wore yesterday, and the day before, and the day before.

I hate to join in with the others, but the food *does* become rather bland. My poor wife has tried to spice up the manna. She has cooked it in a variety of ways. The final straw was when we had manna pizza. Or, as the songwriter put it: manna-cotti (manicotti).

Lesson Four: tombstones are milestones

The Lord has told us, through Moses, that

none of my generation—except Joshua and I—will enter into the Promised Land. In other words, *they* will have to die before *we* can go in. I hate being crass, but the only thing that kept me sane in the Wilderness was waiting upon the members of my generation to die! Honestly, some funerals are more enjoyable than others.

I had the wonderful privilege on one occasion to watch the saddened faces of the families of the ten spies as they dropped dead, in unison, of the plague. I did my best not to shout for joy. Out of respect, I feigned sadness as I put on my "Bill Clinton" face.

You remember the story. Bill and his friend, Tony Campolo, were attending Ron Brown's funeral. Bill and Tony were laughing until Bill looked up and noticed a camera was focused upon him. He changed his countenance immediately into a look of anguish.

I pretended to be sad. I even put on my black cloak for the funeral. But, I must confess, I wasn't really mournful. In fact, I took up "bowling" in their honor.

Methuselah lived to be 969 years old. His name meant, "When he dies, there shall be an emission."[75] An "emission?" Are you kidding me?! It was a worldwide catastrophe!

God, in a wonderful demonstration of His abundant mercy, extended the life of Methuselah as an expression of His desire to give people the opportunity to repent before He sent the Great Flood. In the same way I believed that, as I watched each man and each woman depart, we were edging that much closer to receiving the anachronistic "green light" to go into Canaan.

Lesson Five: friends are few

I know this may seem related to the loneliness I mentioned in lesson three, but this concept is thoroughly distinct. I love Moses; I do. And I always have. But I have never been able to relate to him. He is always much too busy listening to the questions and concerns from the others. I don't want to waste his valuable time.

His brother, Aaron, also seems to be a nice guy. Aaron's greatest problem is that he has always been a people-pleaser; he has always wanted peace at any price. And the price of

---

[75] <u>Enhanced Strong's Lexicon</u>, copyright 1995 Logos Research Systems, Inc.

peace, for me, has always been much too high.

My own immediate family members don't understand me. My wife, my brothers, and my sisters all think I have lost my mind. I tell them, "If you think I'm crazy you will have to get in line—lots of people already think that!" I try to talk to my kids, but they are too busy running around and playing games, like "pin the tail on the camel."

The only person in Israel that I *know* thinks the same way I do is Joshua. He and I have met occasionally to discuss the vision the Lord has given to us. But he really doesn't have much time, either, since he is Moses' servant. Moses keeps him busy.

Lesson Six: you can make progress without progressing

I have been told that there is a significant difference between overcoming and surviving. Most people that encounter difficulties in their lives are satisfied with simply living through an ordeal—of *surviving*. Others, and I would include myself in this group, are overcomers. We will not accept defeat. We are victorious. We will stay close to the Lord, and we will win the battles.

Survivors log the miles along with us, but they merely "exist." They have no joy. And, after time, they begin to appear envious of those that have preceded them in death. Death becomes their welcome friend; for them, "he" cannot come quickly enough.

We overcomers are different. In our minds, every step we take is one step closer to Canaan's land; each day we live is one more day we won't have to wait to enjoy the abundant blessings of God. Our vision, amazingly, becomes clearer with each passing moment.

Lesson Seven: learn to embrace the Wilderness

I have said it before, and I will say it again: "If the world hands you a lemon, make lemonade." Living in the Wilderness hasn't been all bad. For instance, you have plenty of time for such often neglected things as prayer, Bible verse memorization, and meditation. Remember *Rephidim*!

You also have time to rest. You ask, "Rest?

How can you possibly rest when you walk so many miles every day?" I am, of course, referring to an *intellectual* rest. You don't have to think about what you need to do; you simply pick up one foot and then the other. I find the pace in the Wilderness so much more relaxing than the taxing burdens I encountered daily back in the land of Egypt.

Walking has an added benefit. I have discovered that hiking is a really good exercise. And I know that, if I don't stay in shape, I won't be able to fight the giants we will undeniably encounter on the other side of "the River."

Another blessing I have discovered in the Wilderness is the relative insignificance of the things of this world. My energy was previously consumed by competition with my peers for recognition and increasing my wealth. My focus is now, and it took several years to get here, on pleasing God and doing His will.

Ultimately, it all becomes a matter of trust. I believe God has my best interests at heart; He has led me here as a part of His master plan.

Lesson Eight: you will yearn for your new home

I was amazed when I began to hear that many of my compatriots actually wanted to go back to Egypt! Egypt is a picture of the world. We, by God's grace, have been liberated *from* the world. Over time, these people have obviously forgotten the hardships we endured in Egypt. Sure, the food was better there. But the conditions were *much* worse.

Many years from now a wise man, under the inspiration of the Holy Spirit, will pen these words in Philippians 3:13-14:

> *Brethren, I do not regard myself as having laid hold of it yet; but one thing I do: forgetting what lies behind and reaching forward to what lies ahead, I press on toward the goal for the prize of the upward call of God in Christ Jesus.*

I'm not sure who this Jesus is. I believe He may become our Messiah. But I do acknowledge the wisdom of focusing on the future rather than on the past. I have used this axiom, in fact, to forget about Egypt. I have put the previous miles behind me. I have one direction in my life, and that is forward. I am advancing toward the goal that God Himself has placed before me.

In my heart, I have already built my home in Canaan, and I have *decorated* it. I have already seen my daughter's wedding and the birth of my grandchildren. I have envisioned a time of peace after, of course, a season of war. I am ready to go home!

Lesson Nine: God is *always* with you

A teaching assistant in a seminary once noted that, when a group of people split off to form a new church, the new congregation is always named *Emmanuel*: "God is with us!" I don't know about that, but He certainly has been, and continues to be, with me every day of my life.

And the miracles have been too many to count. He has opened up the Red Sea so that we could cross on dry land; He has sent us manna to eat; He has allowed us to survive the bites of poisonous snakes simply by looking upon a bronze serpent called "Nehushtan" — a picture, I am told, of His Son becoming sin on our behalf as

He   will one day be lifted up on a cross.[76] All those that will look upon Him by faith will be saved from the venom of the wicked serpent named Satan.

Lesson Ten: God leads His people through His servants

As I mentioned in lesson nine, the only Israelite among us that knew his way through the Wilderness was Moses. We truly would have been lost without him. You would think, therefore, that God's people would have appreciated him and loyally followed his leadership. But, as you know, they didn't.

I have learned a very important lesson, and several others have learned it along with me: attacking God's servant is tantamount to attacking God! It is no wonder, then, that God so furiously judged the Korahite rebellion.

It just makes sense! As you will learn in the book of Judges, people tend to "do their own thing," and follow their own internal

---

[76] John 3:14.

leadership.[77] But the only way for a large group of people to arrive at the same destination at the same time is for only one solitary person to lead them — in this case, it should have been Moses.

As the pastor of Bellevue Baptist Church, Adrian Rogers will one day say with regard to the husband being the head of the home, "Anything with two heads is a freak; anything with no heads is dead." The same principle holds true for God's people — His church. There is room for one and only one leader; God has clearly given that responsibility to the pastor.

You may have seen the caption on a tee-shirt (another anachronism) that states, "Two things in life are true: 1) there is a God; 2) you're not Him." Maybe churches should issue tee-shirts to the members that state: "1) there is a pastor; 2) you're not him."

The Battles in the Wilderness

Even though (for me) the Wilderness has been, for the most part, without external conflict,

---

[77] Judges 17:6, 21:25.

I have still encountered many internal, spiritual battles. Perhaps you have heard of Don Quixote. I, unfortunately, have not. His story will not be written for centuries yet to come. The poor man, I'm sure you have heard, fought with windmills; he imagined them to be giants.

In contrast to Quixote, my imaginary battles would eventually become real. "Real," you ask. "How can imaginary battles be real?"

I am glad you asked. They are real because they are based upon fact. You see, one day Joshua, the next generation of Israelites, and I will enter into the Promised Land. We will fight real giants and claim real territory from them for ourselves. And, because of my vision from the Lord and the imaginary battles I have fought, I will one day successfully claim my inheritance on the far side of "the River."

All highly trained generals fight imaginary battles. In military circles, this practice is known as "strategizing." Without proper planning, *all* battles will go awry. Just ask Joshua about a little village named "Ai."[78] And you can also ask Nick

---

[78] Joshua 7:1-5.

Saban, coach of the winning team of the 2012 national football championship, about the dangers of underestimating the capabilities of an opponent during his *first* encounter with L.S.U. !

In my most humble, but accurate, opinion, God's primary purpose for the Wilderness is to prepare His people for battle. You don't believe me? Just ask Jesus in a few years at the end of His forty days in the Wilderness. So join with me as I dream about the battles to come.

> God's primary purpose for the Wilderness is to prepare His people for battle.

My Inheritance

We *finally* entered the land, and enjoyed some impressive battles. Everyone was amazed at my ability to fight. I was not surprised. As I have told you, I had been mentally fighting the battles for forty years.

We fought for five full years before Joshua began to divide the land. He called out my name: "Caleb." I pretended to be hard of hearing so that he would say my name again, and then I stepped up. The crowd became silent as I spoke:[79] "Thank you for the birthday card. As most of you know, today is my 85th birthday." Joshua smiled and nodded as I continued, "It has been forty-five years since the day Moses sent twelve spies to survey this land that He has now given to us."

I looked directly at Joshua as I said, "Present company excluded, I alone from my generation have been faithful in following the Lord. Moses recognized my exceptional obedience. He pledged to me and to my children that God would give to us the hill country of Hebron as our rightful inheritance here in Canaan. I am well aware that it is inhabited by giants. I also understand that they live in great walled cities. I realize that, by human standards, I am an old man. But my dream has kept me young. I believe that, if you will honor my request, I will utterly defeat and destroy every single one of those giants."

Joshua may not have liked me; to be honest, by this time I didn't particularly like him, either. But he *did* respect me. He fulfilled my

---

[79] Joshua 14:6-12.

request: "So Joshua blessed [me] and gave Hebron to [me] for an inheritance. Therefore, Hebron became [my] inheritance until this day, because [I] followed the Lord God of Israel fully."[80]

My Epitaph

As I look back upon my life, the greatest thing anyone has ever said about me has been spoken by God Himself! In a statement

contrasting my life with the lives of others, He said in Numbers 14:24:

> *But My servant Caleb, because he has had a different spirit and has followed Me fully, I will bring into the land which he entered, and his descendants shall take possession of it.*

I didn't like the word "but" when Gaddi used it. *BUT* I surely enjoyed hearing it when the

---

[80] Joshua 14:13-14.

Lord said it!

That was the good part; now let me tell you the not-so-good part. Many years from now a man named Paul Simon will write a song entitled, "I Am a Rock."[81] He may well have had me in mind when he penned those words. I have become like a rock, impervious to the needs and the feelings of others. I stand alone.

Have I been successful? I don't really think so. I have been like Abraham's nephew, Lot. I may have *survived* the Wilderness, but I didn't really *overcome* it. I have buried my wife there. I have buried Kenaz and all of my other brothers and sisters there; my parents, grandparents, aunts and uncles, cousins, and, if you can call them that, my "friends." The Lone Ranger had Tonto; I had no one.

Of course, the younger generation survived and entered in with me. My only child, a daughter, came to Hebron with me. I must sadly report that my wife and I had no sons to

---

[81] http://www.paulsimon.com/us/music/paul-simon-songbook/i-am-rock, © 1965 Words and Music by Paul Simon, website visited on 8/28/2011.

carry on the family name.

You ask, "What is your daughter's name?" Her name is "Achsah"; her mother named her. I am almost ashamed to tell you what her name means. It means, "Ankle chain."

You further inquire, "Do you mean like an 'anklet' or 'a piece of jewelry?'" That may have been what her mother meant, but I have always associated her name with the bondage we had experienced while we were slaves in Egypt. But, no matter, Jehovah has set us free!

As my life was coming to a close, I took care of Achsah by ensuring she would have a good husband—a warrior. She would marry the man that could capture Kiriath-sepher. God is good! The claimant was my late brother Kenaz's son, Othniel. Together they will carry on the proud name of Jephunneh. Upon Achsah's request, I gave the young couple a down payment on their inheritance: a field with two springs of water.

The battles, for me, are *finally* over. I have earned the respect of the younger generation. They have seen the "old man" in battle. They have heard the demands I have placed upon

"General" Joshua, and they have seen that he has granted. They have witnessed my rewards, from God Himself, for my years of faithfulness.

My favorite name for God has been Jehovah-nissi. The name means "God my banner"; it "was the title which Moses gave to the altar which he erected on the hill on the top of which he stood with uplifted hands while Israel prevailed over their enemies the Amalekites."[82] As a warrior, I have appreciated the fact that He has been my banner throughout all of the battles of my life.

No one will remember the circumstances of my death — whether it was on the battlefield or on a deathbed. I will let you in on a secret: I died the way I lived. I died *a l o n e*. My motto has been, to quote an early 1900s comedian named W. C. Fields, "Go away kid, you bother me." My secluded tombstone is a constant reminder of my solitude. It says, "Caleb — The Dog — Warrior of

---

[82] Easton, M. G., M. A. D. D., *Easton's Bible Dictionary*, (Oak Harbor, WA: Logos Research Systems, Inc.) 1996.

God."

Whatever you do, "DON'T FOLLOW ME!"

THE SILENT PARTNER

My name is Hoshea, but Moses calls me Joshua. Both names mean the same thing: "Jehovah is salvation." A better name for me would have been דומיה—duwmiyah, which means "the silent one, the still one, the one in repose, the one who is still waiting."

I have become known as the *silent* partner because the Bible only records my words on three occasions: once publicly and twice privately.[83] The first time I spoke occurred right after the twelve of us had returned from our expedition.[84] It was quite a sight! Moses, Aaron, Caleb, and I were standing on one side; the rest of the congregation was standing on the other.

The people had basically announced that they would not enter into the Promised Land.

---

[83] Prior to the book of Joshua.
[84] Numbers 14:5-10.

Following Moses' lead, Aaron, Caleb, and I tore our clothing to express our horror toward their unwillingness to obey God.

I told the people that the land was a wonderful place, and that it was *His* plan for us to possess it. I tried to encourage them not to be afraid. It didn't work. They started making plans to *kill* us. If God hadn't appeared and scared them off, the four of us would have surely been dead!

I also spoke privately on two occasions; both conversations were with Moses. On the first of the two occasions, Moses had invited me to accompany him on his way to the top of Mount Sinai. This was the place where he would spend time communing with God.[85] He left me waiting for forty days at the halfway point. The next time I would see him would be when he was carrying the first set of two tablets containing what we would subsequently call the "Ten Commandments."

I had been listening for days to the sounds emanating from the encampment below. "Moses," I said in my naiveté, "it sounds like

---

[85] Exodus 32:15-20.

there is a fight going on down there." Moses replied, "It sounds more like singing to me."

Moses and I wound our way back down the mountain. And then he saw it: the people had made a calf out of the gold they had brought with them out of Egypt! They were dancing around the idol and conducting acts of extreme immorality. Moses punished them by melting their idol, and crushing it into a fine powder. He poured the granules into a container of water, and made the people drink it. The Levites followed Moses' lead and killed many of the offenders.

The second of my two private conversations came during Moses' appointment of the seventy elders.[86] Sixty-eight of the chosen men had accompanied Moses to the tent of meeting; two of the men had stayed home. The Lord came down in glory. The sixty-eight men began to prophesy: to foretell the wonderful things that God would be doing in our midst.

Suddenly, a boy ran up to me. He handed a note to me that read, "Two men have been caught preaching in another part of the camp." I passed the note to my mentor with my

---

[86] Numbers 11:24-30.

unsolicited commentary: "Moses, you need to do something about this—and the sooner, the better."

Moses read the note and laughed. He asked me, "Are you worried about *my* reputation?" And then he astounded me when he made his next statement: "My wish is that all of God's people would become preachers and be filled with His Holy Spirit." I know Moses' statement probably didn't shock you New Testament believers, since you hold to the concept of the "priesthood of the believer,"[87] but it literally blew me away! You have the privilege, like Moses, of representing God before others as you share your faith, and others before Him as you pray.

I obviously spoke more frequently than on those three recorded occasions, but I did a lot more listening. I'm sure you have heard the adage that was around before I was born: "God gave you two ears and one mouth so that you would listen twice as much as you speak." I have also found that, when *I* talk, I hear what I already know. When you talk and I listen, I can learn

---

[87] 1 Peter 2:9.

what *you* know.

You may have heard the story of a young preacher interrogating an older preacher. The seasoned preacher finally said, "You certainly ask a lot of questions." The young preacher responded, "I decided that, if I learn all that you know and add it to all that I know, I will know more than you." That, my friend, has been my philosophy throughout my personal journey through the Wilderness.

My Résumé

My personal résumé, for your consideration, is as follows:

- I am Moses' servant.
- I am one of the twelve spies selected to explore the Promised Land.
- My name in the Hebrew tongue is ועשיהו — yeh-ho-shoo' ah.
- I will have the unparalleled privilege of sharing my name with the Messiah — the One that will soon come to deliver His people from their sins. You may be more familiar with the Greek spelling and

pronunciation of my name: **Ιησους** (pronounced "ee-ay-sooce" or "Jesus"). That's right. Isn't God good?

- I have served as the commanding general over the Israeli troops in the Wilderness.
- God has used me to finally lead His people out of the Wilderness.

My Mentor

I became known as the silent *partner* because, just as Moses was known as God's servant, I had volunteered to be Moses' servant. My motto has been, "wherever Moses goes, I go."

My commitment to Moses may have been the first of its kind in the Bible, but it is similar to other stories I am sure you have read. Ruth vowed to Naomi:[88]

> *Do not urge me to leave you or turn back from following you; for where you go, I will go, and where you lodge, I will lodge. Your people shall be my people, and your God, my God. Where*

---

[88] Ruth 1:16-17.

*you die, I will die, and there I will be buried.
Thus may the Lord do to me, and worse, if
anything but death parts you and me.*

Elijah gave Elisha several opportunities to
turn back from following him. Elisha refused; he
responded to Elijah, three times, with the words,
"As the Lord lives and as you yourself live, I will
not leave you."[89]

So it was with Moses and me. I was his
"shadow." I patterned my life after Moses. He
spent a great deal of time in the tent of meeting in
the presence of the Lord, and so did I. In fact, on
one occasion, he finished praying and left; I
remained. I figured, "If Moses needs to spend
time with the Lord to prepare for *his* day, I need
even more time alone with the Lord to prepare for
my day!"[90] I am sure it is similar to your
relationship with Jesus Christ. Since He devoted
so much of His time in daily prayer, I know that
you will, too.

My commitment to Moses outlived Moses
himself. Years after his death, I continued to obey

[89] 2 Kings 2:3, 4, 6.
[90] Exodus 33:11.

his instructions. In Joshua 11:12, "[I] captured all the cities of these kings, and all their kings, and [I] struck them with the edge of the sword, and utterly destroyed them; just as Moses the servant of the LORD had commanded [me]."

You may think I am guilty of "Moses-olatry": of, in a sense, deifying Moses. I have never elevated him to the level of worship. He was a great man of God, and he left me a great pattern to follow. I certainly appreciate his leadership in my life. But I have only One that I worship. His name is Jehovah God!

My Ministry

In order to effectively serve the Lord, a minister needs both a *calling* from God and the *confirmation* of men.

God Calls

I assure you that I did not call myself into the ministry. No *true* minister does. After having watched Moses for forty years I had come to one conclusion: a man would have to be crazy to want to serve as a pastor. I am not crazy, at least not *yet*. But I *do* know that God has called me to be His servant.

The details of God's calling upon my life are as follows:[91]

- Moses, our pastor, knew he was going to die, so he prayed that God would send a replacement.
- He specifically asked that his replacement would have the following characteristics:
    - ✓ One of the people; one they already

---

[91] Numbers 27:15-18c.

know and trust.

- ✓ A leader of the people.
- ✓ A shepherd: an associate; a friend.
- ✓ Led by the Holy Spirit of God, and giving evidence of that fact.

Apparently I fit the bill. In response to Moses' prayer, God called me by name. He said in Numbers 27:18b: "Take Joshua the son of Nun."

Man Confirms

Moses began his confirmation of God's calling upon my life by laying his hand upon me.[92] This was the *private* step of my commissioning service. This was a symbolic act. I was *already* filled with the Holy Spirit.

The second step of the service was the *public* segment. I was asked to stand before Eleazar the priest and the rest of the congregation as Moses commissioned me to become his successor. He explained to the congregation that he was transferring a portion of his authority to me so that they would follow me in the same

---

[92] Numbers 27:18d-23.

manner as they had followed him. Moses then
explained to all of us that my greatest
responsibility in leading the people would be to
discern the will of God before making any
decisions; he advised the people that, since I
would be receiving my marching orders from
God, their part would be to do as I commanded
them.

The result of my calling and
commissioning are found in Deuteronomy 34:9b:
"and the sons of Israel listened to [me] and did as
the LORD had commanded Moses."

My Turn to Lead

Moses told us that all of the people twenty
years of age and older would die in the
wilderness. What was their sin? They were
guilty of grumbling and complaining. They
thought they were murmuring against Moses
when they were, in actuality, murmuring against
God. Moses further told the people that Caleb
and I would be the only exceptions.[93]

We have waited for forty years to enter

---

[93] Numbers 14:28-30.

into the Promised Land. We have said our "goodbyes" to all of our friends and relatives. I had, in my own way, said "goodbye" to Moses. What a man! Now it is my turn.

My Two Armies

I have experienced the God-given privilege of leading two armies. One was visible; the other was invisible.

Visible

Moses wasn't kidding when he described the group I would lead into Canaan. Or should I say, what's *left* of the group I would lead into Canaan. God, in His anger, had killed massive numbers of Israelites during our forty-year excursion through the Wilderness! He had prepared me for what I would encounter by saying on five different occasions, both privately and publicly, "Be strong and courageous."

I will never know why God chose to give me such a bunch of misfits to serve in my visible army:[94]

- They are rebellious and stubborn; God will severely judge their rebellion.
- They have continuously rejected God's desire to have a personal relationship with them.
- They have forsaken the Lord; God will, in turn, forsake them.

God tells us, in the book of the Judges, why He uses such undesirable people in His army. Gideon started his campaign against the Midianites with 32,000 warriors. God sent thousands of them home in shifts, until only 300 remained. You ask, "Why did He do *that*?" Look at Judges 7:2: "the people who are with you are too many for me to give Midian into their hands, for Israel would become boastful, saying, 'my own power has delivered me.'"

I now understand. I will give God all of the glory for the amazing victories we will enjoy

---

[94] Deuteronomy 31:16 – 32:43.

in the Promised Land.[95]

Invisible

You may be thinking that I have been out in the sun too long. You may be thinking that I am joking about leading an invisible army. Let me prove it to you. Read the account of Elisha and his servant in 2 Kings 6:15-17:

> *Now when the attendant of the man of God had risen early and gone out, behold, an army with horses and chariots was circling the city. And his servant said to him, "Alas, my master! What shall we do?" So he answered, "Do not fear, for those who are with us are more than those who are with them." Then Elisha prayed and said, "O Lord, I pray, open his eyes that he may see." And the Lord opened the servant's eyes and he saw; and behold, the mountain was*

---

[95] 1 Corinthians 1:26-31.

full of horses and chariots of fire all around Elisha.

Do you believe me now?

Whereas my *visible* army is composed of misfits, my *invisible* army is outstanding! I have served as *Moses'* second in command for forty years; I have now been promoted to *God's* second in command! You don't believe me? Listen to my story.[96]

We had just crossed over "the River." We had circumcised the remaining males in our group and had observed the Feast of the Passover. We had eaten some of the food from the land. And guess what happened? The manna stopped. God was no longer holding our hands and doing everything for us. We were truly entering into a partnership with God. He would now do *through* us what He had formerly done *for* us.

I had not received further instructions from the Lord, so we decided to camp by "the River." I was standing just outside of the land of Jericho. I was minding my own business, when I

---

[96] Joshua 5:10-15.

saw a man standing nearby with a sword in his hand. I thought, "This isn't good." Or, in your vernacular, "Houston, we have a problem."

I was preparing to lead the Israelites into a battle. I asked the man, "Whose side are you on?" His answer was intriguing. He asked, "Whose side are *you* on?" And then He identified Himself: "I am the captain of the host of Heaven. All of the angels are at my personal disposal." In other words, He was claiming to be God. This was another of the many preincarnate appearances of Jesus Christ, our future Messiah.[97]

Something about His voice let me know that His authority was unquestionable. And His eyes—John the Revelator described them well in Revelation 1:14, "his eyes were like a flame of fire."

I bowed before Him. He did not prohibit me from worshiping Him. That fact alone could only mean one thing—I was in the presence of

---

[97] See also Genesis 16:7-11, 22:11-15; Exodus 3:2; Numbers 22:22-35; Judges 2:1-4, 5:23; 6:11-22, 13:3-21; 2 Samuel 24:16; 1 Kings 19:7; 2 Kings 1:3-15, 19:35; 1 Chronicles 21:12-30; Psalms 34:7 and 35:5-6; Isaiah 37:36; Zechariah 1:11-12, 3:1-6, 12:8.

God![98]

I previously had been in a partnership with Moses; I was preparing to enter into a partnership with God. There was only one thing to do—I asked Him, "What do you want *me* to do? I want to be on *Your* side."

Reminiscent of Jesus' first meeting with Moses, He told me to take off my shoes; I complied.[99] The reason: I was standing on holy ground. You ask, "What is holy ground?" I believe it is the place where you first meet with God; it can also be any other place *where*, or any other time *when*, you meet with God. In other words, you might as well remain shoeless. All ground is His; all ground, therefore, is holy.

Do you remember the story of the Roman centurion that approached Jesus to ask him to heal his servant?[100] Of course *I* don't; the incident won't occur for hundreds of years. Jesus offered to go to the centurion's house to pray for the servant. The centurion said that it wouldn't be necessary; he understood that Jesus had willingly

---

[98] Acts 10:26, 14:11-15; Revelation 19:10, 22:8-9.
[99] Exodus 3:5.
[100] Matthew 8:5-13.

placed Himself under the authority of His Heavenly Father. As a result, Jesus had access to the authority of His Father. He could simply issue the command, and it would be done.

In the same way, by placing myself under the authority of my Captain, the Lord Jesus Christ, I would become His lieutenant. Every time I have listened to His orders and have obeyed His leadership, I have effectively become the leader of *His* invisible army — *my* invisible army — the angels of Heaven.

As you read our exploits in the book that bears my name, you will see numerous victories that cannot be explained by human effort alone. Need I say more? I have enjoyed the privilege of leading two armies: one visible; the other invisible.

My Two Enemies

I will face four battles prior to leading the

people across "the River."

My First Enemy — Leisure

Perhaps you have heard of the "Battle of Rephidim?" It is the only battle conducted by the original generation in the Wilderness. It was the inevitable result, in God's economy, of the despicable practices of the ankle-biting Amalekites.

Moses has already told you that Rephidim means "resting places." Moses was exhausted, and the people were also becoming fatigued. We had stopped to rest. B I G mistake! There in our resting place we encountered Amalek. Amalek was the grandson of Esau, our ancestor's, Jacob's brother. The Amalekites had perfected the technique of waiting until our warriors had passed them by. They would then attack the old, the sick, and the tired people at the rear terminus of our procession. Amalek would sneak up behind them, kill them, and take their possessions.

Moses instructed me to lead the fight while

he, his brother Aaron, and Hur remained on the top of the hill overlooking the battle. This was, however, a most unusual battle. The ground troops had little to do with the outcome. As long as Moses held up the rod of God in his hand, we were victorious; whenever he lowered his hand, we experienced defeat.

I learned three lessons that day. First, the battle belongs to the Lord — He Himself fights on our behalf.[101]

Second, I also learned the value of "holding up my leader's hands." I have since made a commitment to pray daily for Moses.

Third, I further learned the dangers of stopping to rest. Amalek would never have been able to ambush us if we had continued moving forward on our predetermined path through the Wilderness. We are on a journey — we can never afford to stop progressing, therefore, until we arrive at our final destination. The bottom line:

---

[101] 1 Samuel 17:47.

when you rest, you die.

My Second Enemy — Satan

You readers have the advantage of knowing that Jesus spent forty days in the Wilderness prior to the inauguration of His earthly ministry — one day for every year we lived there. At the end of the forty days, Satan (the Adversary, the Accuser, the Unseen Foe) met with Him. Satan had one purpose: to block Jesus' path; to change His direction; to keep Him from accomplishing His Father's mission.[102]

In the same way, we Israelites encountered Satan — *our* Unseen Foe — at the end of our Wilderness wanderings. Why would he choose to wait to attack us *now*? Why didn't he oppose us before? The reason is that we, as Wilderness dwellers, were not a significant threat to him and his kingdom.

But those that enter the Promised Land — they are an extremely *dangerous* group! We were about to enter *his* territory — *his* kingdom. And so

---

[102] Luke 4:1-13.

he placed several enemies along our path in a last-ditch effort to impede our progress. Join me as I reminisce upon two battlefields in which we encountered Satan—the visible front and the invisible one.

The Visible Battlefront

The visible battlefront consisted of three skirmishes: the Battle of the Negev, the Battle of Heshbon, and the Battle of Bashan.

The first visible battleground has become known as the "Battle of the Negev."[103] The king of Arad heard we were coming his way. He issued orders for his people to fight with us; they took some of our people as prisoners. Moses prayed and we cried out to the Lord. The tide of the battle quickly turned; we stopped retreating and began to advance upon the Aradites.

We named the place *Hormah*, which means "devotion." We dedicated the land to the Lord. And we did what we *should* have done in all of

---

[103] Numbers 21:1-3.

our subsequent battles: we took *no* prisoners; we destroyed *all* of their cities.

Note to my readers: NEVER compromise with your enemies; you will learn their ways and thus abandon the ways of the Lord.

We called the second visible battleground the "Battle of Heshbon."[104] We only wanted to pass through the land of the Amorites. We had no plans of stopping there to eat or to drink; we promised to keep moving our procession constantly forward on the main highway. We sent a message to their king outlining our request. He replied, "No — you will have to find another route."

And then the king sent his entire army to attack us. That was a big mistake — we had the Lord and His army of angels on our side! We captured all of the cities of the Amorites, and crossed the land on what has now become *our* new highway.

The third and final visible battleground was the "Battle of Bashan."[105] We left the land of the Amorites and proceeded toward a district

---

[104] Numbers 21:21-26.
[105] Numbers 21:33-35.

known as Bashan. Their king, Og, assembled his troops for battle. Moses inquired of the Lord; God told him that He was going to give us this land also—this "fruitful" land—for our possession. He told Moses, "Just as I have defeated Heshbon, I will also defeat Bashan." We won the victory and, once again, took no

> Remember: NEVER compromise with your enemies; you will learn their ways and abandon the ways of the Lord. (Not only that—their surviving offspring will one day rise up and get you!)

prisoners.

The Invisible Battlefront

Having failed to dissuade us on three visible fronts from the final leg of our journey, Satan resorted to his most effective tactic: attacking us *spiritually*. He knew that if he could obstruct our intimacy with God, he would successfully block our path; he would turn us back into the Wilderness.

NOTE: Satan still attacks church members today whenever he perceives they are preparing to cross "the River" into the land of the Spirit-filled Christian life.

The fourth campaign, the "Battle of Midian," would be the only *invisible* battlefront and the only *offensive* battle we would wage as we made our final preparations to cross "the River."[106]

Balak, the Moabite king, had learned of Israel's prowess on the battlefield. He had likely heard of the defeat of the Amalekites, so an ambush from the rear was out of the question. He certainly didn't want to launch a full frontal attack. What would he do? Remember that the real enemy on the invisible battlefront is Satan. How would *he* attack us? He would utilize the following grocery

> Satan still attacks church members today whenever he perceives they are preparing to cross "the River" into the land of the Spirit-filled Christian life.

---

[106] Numbers 31:1-54.

list of sins:

- **Self-reliance** — Matthew 4:3-4: "And the tempter came and said to Him, 'If You are the Son of God, command that these stones become bread.' But He answered and said, 'It is written, *Man shall not live on bread alone, but on every word that proceeds out of the mouth of God.'"*

- **Presumptuousness** — Matthew 4:5-7: "Then the devil took Him into the holy city and had Him stand on the pinnacle of the temple, and said to Him, 'If You are the Son of God, throw Yourself down; for it is written, *He will command His angels concerning You; and on their hands they will bear You up*, so that *You will not strike Your foot against a stone.'* Jesus said to him, 'On the other hand, it is written, *You shall not put the Lord your God to the test.'"*

- **Idolatry** — Matthew 4:8-11: "Again, the devil took Him to a very high mountain and showed Him all the kingdoms of the world and their glory; and he said to Him, 'All these things I will give You, if You fall down and worship me.' Then Jesus said to him, 'Go, Satan! For it is written, *You shall worship the Lord your God, and serve Him only.'* Then the devil left Him; and behold, angels came and began to minister to Him."

- **Obstruction**—Matthew 16:23: "But He turned and said to Peter, 'Get behind Me, Satan! You are a stumbling block to Me; for you are not setting your mind on God's interests, but man's.'"

- **Apostasy**—Luke 22:31-32: "Simon, Simon, behold, Satan has demanded permission to sift you like wheat; but I have prayed for you, that your faith may not fail; and you, when once you have turned again, strengthen your brothers."

- **Unforgiveness**—2 Corinthians 2:10-11: "But one whom you forgive anything, I forgive also; for indeed what I have forgiven, if I have forgiven anything, I did it for your sakes in the presence of Christ, so that no advantage would be taken of us by Satan, for we are not ignorant of his schemes."

- **Anger** — Ephesians 4:26-27: "Be angry, and yet do not sin; do not let the sun go down on your anger, and do not give the devil an opportunity."
- **Rebellion** — James 4:7: "Submit therefore to God. Resist the devil and he will flee from you."
- **Pride** — 1 Peter 5:6-8: "Therefore humble yourselves under the mighty hand of God, that He may exalt you at the proper time, casting all your anxiety on Him, because He cares for you. Be of sober spirit, be on the alert. Your adversary, the devil, prowls around like a roaring lion, seeking someone to devour."

We Israelites have gone through the checkout line at the devil's supermarket, and have paid dearly for the contents of our shopping cart!

Before we could fight the external enemy, we had to defeat the enemy within. This came to be known as the "sin of Peor."[107] Many of our men had been seduced by Midianite women. In

---

[107] Numbers 25:1-9.

conjunction with their immorality, they had also worshiped the false god of the Midianites. They were, for all intents and purposes, worshiping Satan himself!

Moses ordered the leaders of Israel to execute all of the men that had been involved in idol worship. The leaders obeyed. God, on His part, sent a plague that took the lives of 24,000 more of our people.

Once we had purged the enemy from within, we were ready to fight the external enemy — the Midianites.[108] I led 12,000 men into battle. We certainly didn't want to leave the Lord out of *this* battle, so Phinehas the priest accompanied us. Our objective: every Midianite man must die and every city utterly destroyed.

We fully obeyed Moses — or so we *thought*. He discovered that we had compromised with our enemies. Moses gave us one final assignment: to kill *all* of the male Midianite children and *all* of the females (except those that were still virgins).

We carried out our orders, and Moses was

---

[108] Numbers 31:1-12.

pleased. It would become his final act as the leader of our people.[109]

My Epitaph

Caleb has told you that God's primary purpose for the Wilderness is to prepare His people for battle. In a sense, he was correct. I would, however, put it this way: God's primary purpose for the Wilderness has always been to form a lasting partnership with His people.

> God's primary purpose for the Wilderness has always been to form a lasting partnership with His people.

My favorite name for God has been Jehovah-sabbaoth, meaning, "The Lord of Hosts." I met Jesus, the captain of the angels, at the riverside. He has been, throughout the years, my ever-present partner.

Some of my last recorded words have been appropriately inscribed on my tombstone: "But as for me and my house, we will serve the

---

[109] Numbers 31:2.

LORD."[110]

Joshua

I believe that, since I have followed Him, God is

---

[110] Joshua 24:15.

inviting you to:

"FOLLOW ME!"

Or, as Paul said in 1 Corinthians 11:1: "Follow my example, as I follow the example of Christ."[111]

---

[111] Scripture taken from the Holy Bible, NEW INTERNATIONAL VERSION®. Copyright © 1973, 1978, 1984 by Biblica, Inc. All rights reserved worldwide. Used by permission.

CONCLUSIONS

My mother (the author's mother) grew up on a farm in South Georgia. My father used to say (jokingly) that he met her "on the north end of a southbound mule." One thing is certain: the view from that vantage point rarely changes!

"The north end" is an apt description of the Wilderness. Israel marched around in the same set tribal order day after day, viewing the same scenery year after year. My question for you, my dear reader, is, "How could anyone remain satisfied in *that* environment for forty years?" For some, the answer is that they are unaware that God is offering them an alternative; for others, they actually seem to *prefer* the eternal sameness of the Wilderness.

You will discover that the two most miserable congregations are Wilderness churches led by Promised Land pastors and leaders, and

Promised Land churches led by Wilderness pastors and leaders. They cannot seem to coexist for any length of time. There is one basic reason: their response to change. Wilderness dwellers repudiate change; Promised Land dwellers embrace it.

What are some conclusions, some takeaways, we can glean from our time together in the Wilderness? And what can you look forward to as you enter the Promised Land?

The Wilderness

- The Holy Spirit *will* lead you into the Wilderness.
- You should enjoy your time in the Wilderness. It is a time of getting to know the Lord more intimately as He provides for your every need.
- Don't plan on staying too long. The Christian life is much more fulfilling when you form a partnership with God.
- Most American churches may be described as "Wilderness churches." They have long since forgotten their purpose;

they have lost their vision; they are simply wandering around in circles, accomplishing little of kingdom value.

- As with Israel, the age of the membership seems to be a factor. A church that has a membership with a median age of fifty years or more is much more likely to remain in the Wilderness than one with a median age of thirty years.

- An *established* church, one that has been in existence for fifty or more years, is much more likely to remain in the Wilderness than one that has been more recently organized.

- God, through His prophets and preachers, has given every generation of believers a "taste" of His glory. Those people that choose to reject it and flee back into the Wilderness will never again have the opportunity to return to the Land of Promise.[112] They will become perennial

---

[112] Hebrews 6:4-8.

Wilderness dwellers.

The Promised Land

- Perennial Wilderness dwellers, those that refuse to leave the Wilderness, will oppose you as you prepare to cross "the River." An interesting article that describes their motivation is "Crabs in a Barrel Syndrome: Will It Ever End?"[113]

- The Promised Land represents the Spirit-filled Christian life; it is *not* a picture of Heaven. It is inhabited by imperfect people and is not, therefore, a perfect place.

- The greatest challenge you will face in the Promised Land will be a tendency to

---

[113] Melody T. McCloud, M.D., "Crabs in a Barrel Syndrome: Will it ever end? Don't crawl over and compete; instead, celebrate each other." Published on March 21, 2011 in Black Women's Health and Happiness, reprinted at http://www.psychologytoday.com/blog/black-womens-health-and-happiness/201103/crabs-in-barrel-syndrome-will-it-ever-end, site visited on 9/16/2011.

compromise with the Enemy — Satan. You will mistakenly believe that you can handle him; you will imagine that you and he can tolerate one another. Remember: "Whenever [the devil] speaks a lie, he speaks from his own nature, for he is a liar and the father of lies."[114]   Your motto needs to become: "Take no prisoners!"

- The age-based stereotype is not necessarily etched in stone. Older men and women are also capable of embracing God's plan and crossing "the River" into the Promised Land. The prophet stated in Joel 2:28: "It will come about after this that I will pour out My Spirit on all mankind; and your sons and daughters will prophesy, your old men will dream dreams, your young men will see visions."

One final word: you have been given only one shot at this life. Make it count, pray *diligently*, select your pathway *carefully*, and watch *whom* you follow!

---

[114] John 8:44b.

PREFERENCE CHART

Wilderness dwellers prefer:	Promised Land dwellers prefer:
A pastor, or civilian leader: Moses	A general, or military leader: Joshua
To be led by the flesh—personal choices	To be led by the Holy Spirit—God's choices
To receive welfare from God	To work in a partnership with God
To resist all change; reject it	To accept and embrace change; welcome it
To remain internally focused: resources expended upon the membership	To become externally focused: resources expended upon the community and the world

Wilderness dwellers prefer:	Promised Land dwellers prefer:
To wander around aimlessly — plateaued or declining membership	To constantly look for more territory to conquer — people to win to Christ, land to buy, buildings to build, organization to enlarge
Safety; low tolerance for risk	Adventure; high tolerance for risk
Comfort; peace at all costs	Conflict, confrontation as needed
To avoid spiritual warfare: Satan doesn't exist	To seek spiritual warfare: Satan must be defeated
The broad way that leads to destruction[115]	The narrow way that leads to life

---

[115] Matthew 7:13-14.

BIBLIOGRAPHY

Easton, M. G., M. A. D. D., *Easton's Bible
    Dictionary*, (Oak Harbor, WA: Logos
    Research Systems, Inc.) 1996.

Enhanced Strong's Lexicon, copyright 1995
    Logos Research Systems, Inc.

George, Timothy, and Denise George, gen. eds.,
    Payday Someday and Other Sermons by
    Robert Greene Lee, (Nashville: Broadman
    and Holman Publishers, 1995), pg. 48.

Harris, R. Laird, Gleason L. Archer, Jr., and
    Bruce K. Waltke, eds., Theological
    Wordbook of the Old Testament,
    (Chicago: Moody Press, 1980).

http://churchgrowth1.blogspot.com/2007/07/top-ten-criticisms-from-church-and.html, site visited on 8/25/2011.

http://evolution.berkeley.edu/evosite/evo101/IIIC6aOntogeny.shtml, site visited on 8/27/2011.

http://www.cabcollege.org/site/user/files/Psalm%20100_The%20Sheep%20of%20His%20Pasture.pdf, site visited on 8/30/2011.

http://www.countryhumor.com/redneck/mightbe.htm, site visited on 8/25/2011.

http://www.paulsimon.com/us/music/paul-simon-songbook/i-am-rock, © 1965 Words and Music by Paul Simon, website visited on 8/28/2011.

http://www.psychologytoday.com/blog/black-womens-health-and-appiness/201103/crabs-in-barrel-syndrome-will-it-ever-end, site visited on 9/16/2011."Crabs in a Barrel Syndrome: Will it ever end?Don't crawl over and compete; instead, celebrate each other."Published on March 21, 2011 by Melody T. McCloud, M.D. in Black Women's Health and Happiness.

OTHER BOOKS BY W. SCOTT MOORE

Supernatural Strategy
(Now available through Eleos Press)

Have you ever tried to share your faith with an unbeliever? It can be, to say the least, extremely challenging. This difficulty is heightened by the fact that Satan wants to keep people in their un-saved condition. This book has been written as an aid to assist the reader in binding the influence of the Unseen Foe and all of the minions of Hell so that he or she can more effectively present the Gospel of Jesus Christ.

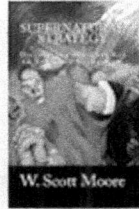

Uganda's Messianic Muslim
(Now available through Eleos Press)

Nassan Ibrahim, formerly a Muslim, has surrendered his life to the Lord Jesus Christ. He is a powerful preacher of the Word of God. He has raised hundreds of thousands of dol-lars for ministries ranging from a radio station, orphanages for Ugandan children left homeless as a result of AIDS, constructing church buildings, and spon-soring the ministries of other Ugandan pastors.

www.ingramcontent.com/pod-product-compliance
Lightning Source LLC
Chambersburg PA
CBHW070954040426

42443CB00007B/504